GEORGE AND MARINA
DUKE AND DUCHESS OF KENT

CHRISTOPHER WARWICK

Original version of *George and Marina, Duke and Duchess of Kent*, first
published by Weidenfeld & Nicolson in 1988
This revised edition published by Albert Bridge Books 2016
Copyright © Christopher Warwick 2016

Cover photograph of Prince George and Princess Marina, Duke and Duchess
of Kent on their wedding day (cropped version of the original) by Alexander
Bassano. Courtesy of Royal Collection Trust/© Her Majesty Queen Elizabeth II
2016

ISBN-13: 978-1-909771-15-4

AUTHOR'S NOTE

In 1988, *George and Marina, Duke and Duchess of Kent,* the biography I had been commissioned to write to commemorate the twentieth anniversary of the death of Princess Marina was published.

This revised and in large part re-written book, which also includes additional material, though based on my earlier study will, I hope, stand alone in re-telling the story of a prince and princess who in the 1930s – high society's 'golden age' - were considered to be the nation's most glamorous royal couple. And so they were, though theirs was a marriage that was tragically cut short during the Second World War when Prince George was killed in what is still regarded as a mysterious flying accident.

At the time of writing the first book, I was most grateful for the assistance I received from many first-hand sources, not all of whom wished to be acknowledged by name. The thanks I extended then, however, though not all concerned are still alive, are every bit as valid today, for what helped to form the basis of that first study has also shaped, informed and influenced this. Among those whose assistance I especially valued were John Cavanagh, Robin Macwhirter, Lady Elizabeth Anson, HRH Princess Juliana of the Netherlands, Lady Alexandra Metcalfe, Mona Mitchell (Private Secretary to HRH Princess Alexandra), Hugo Vickers, Jean Auld, Michael Bloch, Jeremy Silver and John Westmancoat (National Sound Archives, London), Kira Karageorgevitch (Princess Kira zu Leiningen), Audrey Whiting, Lily Wheeler, Clifford Wade, R.J. Evans, Frank FitzGerald-Bush, Brian Auld, Alex MacCormick, Valerie Garner,

Charlotte Balazs; the Lord Chamberlain's Office, the archivists of the Franklin D. Roosevelt Library, New York, and the staff of the reference sections at the United States Embassy in London, the Greek Embassy, and the India Office Library. Today, by way of thanks for further advice and assistance, I must also add fellow writer and journalist Christopher Wilson, and Charlotte Howard and Chelsey Fox.

Christopher Warwick
2015

Russian and Greek Royal Families

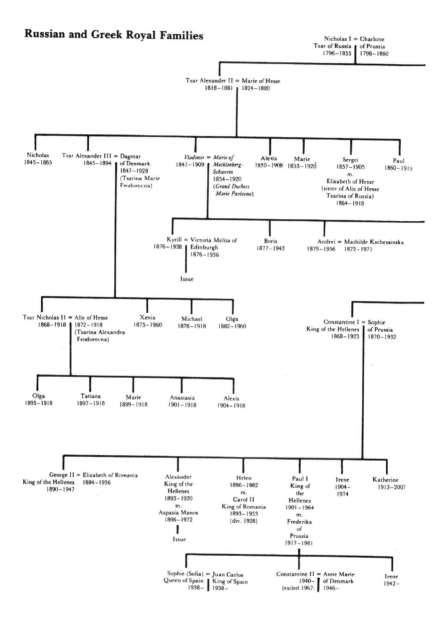

Nicholas I = Charlotte
Tsar of Russia | of Prussia
1796–1855 | 1798–1860

Tsar Alexander II = Marie of Hesse
1818–1881 | 1824–1880

Nicholas
1843–1865

Tsar Alexander III = Dagmar
1845–1894 | of Denmark
1847–1928
(Tsarina Marie
Feodorovna)

Vladimir = Marie of
1847–1909 | Mecklenberg-
Schwerin
1854–1920
(Grand Duchess
Marie Pavlovna)

Alexis
1850–1908

Marie
1853–1920

Sergei
1857–1905
m.
Elisabeth of Hesse
(sister of Alix of Hesse
Tsarina of Russia)
1864–1918

Paul
1860–1919

Kyrill = Victoria Melita of
1876–1938 | Edinburgh
1876–1936

Boris
1877–1943

Andrei = Mathilde Kschessinska
1879–1956 | 1872–1971

Issue

Tsar Nicholas II = Alix of Hesse
1868–1918 | 1872–1918
(Tsarina Alexandra
Feodorovna)

Xenia
1875–1960

Michael
1878–1918

Olga
1882–1960

Constantine I = Sophie
King of the Hellenes | of Prussia
1868–1923 | 1870–1932

Olga
1895–1918

Tatiana
1897–1918

Marie
1899–1918

Anastasia
1901–1918

Alexis
1904–1918

George II = Elizabeth of Romania
King of the Hellenes | 1894–1956
1890–1947

Alexander
King of the
Hellenes
1893–1920
m.
Aspasia Manos
1896–1972

Issue

Helen
1896–1982
m.
Carol II
King of Romania
1893–1953
(div. 1928)

Paul I
King of
the
Hellenes
1901–1964
m.
Frederika
of
Prussia
1917–1981

Irene
1904–
1974

Katherine
1913–2007

Sophie (Sofia) = Juan Carlos
Queen of Spain | King of Spain
1938– | 1938–

Constantine II = Anne Marie
1940– | of Denmark
(exiled 1967; | 1946–

Irene
1942–

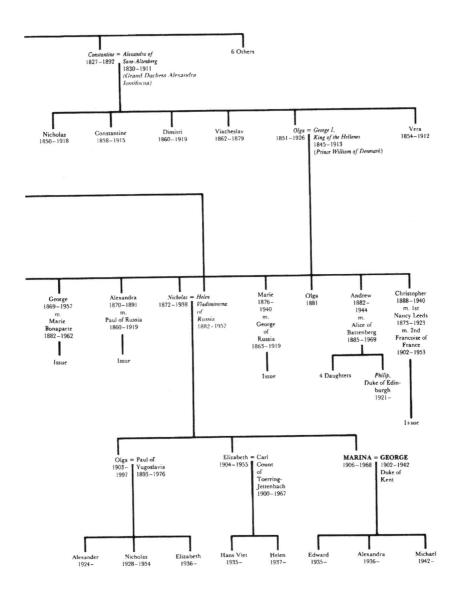

CONTENTS

CHAPTER ONE
ROMANOV INHERITANCE

Tsarskoe Selo, or Tsar's Village, known today as Pushkin in honour of Russia's national poet, is located 24-kilometres south of St Petersburg. For 200 years, ever since Peter the Great's wife Catherine first built a modest stone house there in 1718, it had been a favourite summer retreat of the imperial Romanovs. Less than forty years after that first house was built, the empress Elisabeth Petrovna decided something far grander and far more imperial was to be created. And so to the designs of Francesco Bartolomeo Rastrelli, senior court architect, the Great Catherine Palace, or Yekaterininsky Dvorets, arose embodying every extravagant mood and opulent nuance of the Baroque school.

Hovering over the roof line at the northern extreme of the palace's 325-meter long facade, itself ornamented with rows of towering columns, gilded window surrounds and wrought-iron balconies, a cluster of five onion domes, each one gilded with solid gold leaf, rose above the chapel, otherwise known as the Church of the Resurrection, that Elisabeth Petrovna had incorporated into the palace. It was in this church that the story of Princess Marina, Duchess of Kent, may be said to have its genesis. For it was here, according to the long and solemn rites of the Russian Orthodox Church, that her parents were married on 29 August 1902.

Princess Marina's father, Prince Nicholas of Greece, born on 27 January 1872, was the third son and fourth child of the Danish-born King George I of the Hellenes and his Russian wife, Olga. The grandson of King Christian IX and Queen Louise of Denmark, Prince Nicholas was also the nephew of Britain's Queen Alexandra, consort of King Edward VII, and her sisters Thyra, who was both Duchess of Cumberland and Duchess of Brunswick-Luneburg, and Dagmar who, as the Tsarina Marie

Feodorovna, consort of Tsar Alexander III, would be Russia's penultimate empress.

Prince Nicholas's bride on that hot summer's day long ago was the Grand Duchess Yelena Vladimirovna of Russia. Known as 'Ellen', she was a niece of Tsar Alexander III and first cousin of his ill-fated son, Nicholas II. Her father was Grand Duke Vladimir Alexandrovich, third son of the assassinated 'Tsar-Liberator' Alexander II. Described as 'handsome and imperious', with a ruddy complexion, loud voice and fierce temper (so fierce that it often terrified his nephew, the young tsar Nicholas), Vladimir was not only 'a great hunter and a gourmet', but as president of the Imperial Academy, also a lover of literature and the arts. In August 1874, he had married his second cousin, Duchess Marie of Mecklenburg-Schwerin, daughter of Grand Duke Frederick Francis II and Princess Augusta of Reuss-Köstritz, the first of his three wives. Known as Grand Duchess Marie Pavlovna, 'Miechen' as she was called within the family, was ambitious and strong-willed. In St Petersburg, within the gilded surroundings of the Vladimir Palace, overlooking the broad expanse of the River Neva, Marie Pavlovna, who was regarded by many as the grandest of all the grand duchesses, established a reputation as being among the best, if not *the* best, of high society hostesses, presiding over a glittering Court that eclipsed that of Nicholas II and his anti-social empress Alexandra, and rivalled that of Nicholas's mother, Marie Feodorovna. A commanding personality, Grand Duchess Vladimir ranked as the third lady in the empire, coming immediately after the two empresses with whom, like her husband, she always had a lukewarm, precariously balanced personal relationship.

Grand Duchess 'Ellen', the Vladimir's only daughter, who had been born on 17 January 1882, a decade almost to the very day after Prince Nicholas, was, to quote her husband, 'lovely and fascinating'. Yet, as she grew older, she became every bit as grand and imperious as her mother, only too aware of her standing as both an imperial and royal highness. Her lofty attitude was something that did nothing to endear her to other royal figures, including two British monarchs, Kings George V and George VI. But at the time of their marriage, Prince Nicholas described himself as 'the proud winner of a lovely bride who had won for herself a place in all hearts by her sweet nature and unselfishness'.

The marriage of Prince and Princess Nicholas of Greece forged yet another link in an intricate, Europe-wide royal web: a web that once again tied the Russian imperial house of Romanov with the network of royal families that, until the end of the Great War, dominated Europe's political and social structure. Of his immediate family, Prince Nicholas not only followed the example of his sisters Alexandra (who became the first wife of Grand Duke Paul Alexandrovich) and Marie (whose first husband was Grand Duke George Mikhailovich), in marrying a Romanov but, more notably, that of his father, King George I of Greece. Moreover, if in 1902, as he would claim in his memoirs *My Fifty Years,* published in 1928, Nicholas felt 'conscience-stricken' at taking his wife away from her family, to say nothing of the splendour of her life in imperial Russia, then his sentiments undoubtedly echoed those of the young King George little more than thirty years earlier.

Unlike the Russian monarchy which celebrated its tercentenary not long before revolution destroyed the institution along with 17 members of the Romanov family in 1918, the Greek monarchy was of relatively recent origin, dating back only to 1832 with the accession to the throne of a newly independent Greece, of Prince Otto of Bavaria. His despotic rule, however, would provoke two revolutions. With his final deposition in 1863, the eighteen-year-old Prince William of Denmark was elected to the Greek throne, which he ascended as King George I. Four years later, the young sovereign travelled to St Petersburg to visit his sister Dagmar, now Grand Duchess Marie Feodorovna, who had recently married the future Tsar Alexander III. While he was there he again met Grand Duchess Olga Konstantinovna, the eldest daughter of Grand Duke Konstantine Nikolaievich, a brother of Tsar Alexander II, and his wife, the former Princess Alexandra of Saxe-Altenburg. Aged twelve when they were first introduced, Olga who was now almost sixteen (and still in the classroom), fell in love with George. The feeling was mutual and although her father thought she was still a little too young for marriage, gave his consent to George's proposal.

The marriage of George I and the young Grand Duchess Olga took place in the chapel at the Winter Palace on 15/27 October 1867 amid celebrations that lasted for five days. After a short honeymoon at Ropsha, an imperial estate south-west of St Petersburg, the new queen of Greece, whose youth was emphasized by the trunk full of dolls she took with her, was on her way to a new country and a new people. In time, King George's child bride would become one of Greece's best-loved queens. She, in turn, developed a lasting affection for the volatile nation over which her husband had been chosen to rule. Yet throughout a long and eventful life, one that included raising a family of five sons and two daughters, Queen Olga always felt homesick, pining, especially during the early years, not just for the company of her own family but for Russia itself. Indeed, it was said that leaving the land of her birth filled the queen with a profound and permanent sense of loss.

Fortunately for the 'conscience' of King George and Queen Olga's son Nicholas, the twenty-year-old Grand Duchess Yelena Vladimirovna did not experience so profound a sense of loss when she married and surrendered the security of her homeland for a simpler, more primitive way of life in Greece. But like her mother-in-law before her, the new Princess Nicholas, as she became, could not avoid discovering some of the more obvious disadvantages of life in Athens. The royal palace, for example, where she and her husband spent the first three years of their married life was old-fashioned, uncomfortable and draughty; a house in which only two bathrooms served more than 300 rooms, and where cockroaches were more likely to spill from the bath taps than clean water.

By contrast, the discomfort Prince and Princess Nicholas experienced at the royal palace was alleviated by the regular visits they made to Tatoi, King George's 40,000-acre estate some twenty-seven kilometres outside Athens. Situated on the densely wooded south-east facing slope of Mount Parnitha, Tatoi was to the Greek royal family what Balmoral was and still is to their British royal relations – a private retreat. In his memoirs Prince Nicholas wrote, 'Of all the places where I have lived, either in Greece or any other country, Tatoi will always stand out as the dwelling round which are centred the happiest recollections of my life as a child and as a man. For my parents, as well as for us children, Tatoi represented our real home – the place that belonged to us, where everyone was free to do as he liked. For my parents it meant a rest in their life devoted to its many duties.... For us it represented liberty, independence, the scene of our wildest romps and frolics.'

It was at Tatoi on 11 June 1903, shortly before she and her husband celebrated their first wedding anniversary, that Princess Nicholas gave birth to the eldest of their three daughters, whom they named Olga in tribute to her paternal grandmother. A second daughter, Elizabeth, was born almost a year later on 24 May 1904. Yet if those confinements had both gone well, that of their third and youngest daughter, Marina, on 13 December 1906, proved to be a particularly harrowing experience, as much for the anguished father as for the mother herself. In his memoirs Prince Nicholas chose to reveal little about the circumstances surrounding his youngest child's birth, save to say that after Marina's delivery, Princess Nicholas had been 'so seriously ill' that he 'lived through moments of terrible anguish'. For a long time, he wrote, the princess had been 'so fragile that she could take little or no part in public life', adding that for two years running, she had undertaken 'a treatment' at the famous Franzensbad health spa, near Prague. Many years later, however, Prince Nicholas would say of his youngest – and, some claim, his favourite – daughter, 'She was a very dear baby. She nearly cost her mother her life'.

Unlike her sisters, Princess Marina – who was named at the suggestion of her grandfather King George I after 'one of the best loved of all Greek saints' – was born not at Tatoi, but at the newly completed Nicholas Palace in Athens, where her parents had taken up residence late in 1905. This imposing whitewashed house – more mansion than palace – had been built for Prince and Princess Nicholas as a wedding present from Tsar Alexander III, the princess's uncle. Today the home of the Italian Embassy, the palace was set in a garden shaded by fig trees and brimming with oleander and bougainvillea, its interior furnished with the treasures the discerning Prince Nicholas had personally collected. Yet, not only was the two-storey house considered to be the most elegant building of its kind in all Athens, it was also the height of modernity and the envy of all, installed with such luxuries as central heating, hot and cold running water and bathrooms that were fitted with heated towel rails.

Until revolution scattered the Greek royal family in 1917, life for Prince Nicholas, his wife and daughters was as close to perfection as it was possible to get. If in retrospect, therefore, Princess Marina's childhood seemed bathed in perpetual sunlight there would be events in her later life that would inevitably be far less blissful. 'She is a child of destiny, and there will be both sunshine and shadows for her,' a gypsy woman is said to have foretold when Marina was but a few months old. 'She will be beautiful and make a great marriage with a king's son. Love will be her guiding star. It will bring her sorrow, for she will lose her husband while she is still young and at the height of her happiness. But she will find consolation in her children.'

Though Princess Nicholas was devoted to each of her daughters, her idea of motherhood stopped short at breastfeeding. That task was entrusted to local peasant women who were engaged as wet nurses. Once they were weaned, the children's welfare became the responsibility of their redoubtable, 33-year-old, Norland-trained nanny, Miss Kate Fox. The Middlesex-born daughter of a newspaper publisher, who, save for an absence of eight years, would remain with the family as nurse or assistant/companion for the rest of her life, spoon-fed the princesses camomile tea, sponged their bodies with cold sea water, encouraged physical exercise and, as her three charges reached the toddler stage, allowed them to play virtually naked in the garden of their home. 'My poor father was in despair and predicted that their complexions would be ruined forever when he saw these children become as brown as berries,' Prince Nicholas would recall. But English practices insisted on by a typically English nanny won the whole-hearted support of Prince and Princess Nicholas, both champions of the English way of life, despite the anxious protests of both sets of grandparents, used to swaddling their offspring in unnecessary layers of clothing, and allowing them out into the sunshine only if suitably attired and protected by parasols and lace-trimmed bonnets, or both.

Radical though Kate Fox's methods of raising children may have seemed to some, their practical benefits were always much in evidence during the development of Princess Marina and her elder sisters. It was also due partly to the efforts of 'Foxy', as she was known to the family, that an operation in 1911 to straighten Marina's left foot proved such a success. At birth – and this may perhaps give some indication of the difficulties Princess Nicholas experienced in what might well have been a breech birth – it was discovered that Marina's left leg was not only thinner and a little shorter than the right, but that her left foot had been twisted to one side. It was even asserted that the foot was badly misshapen as a result. Be that as it may, Foxy massaged the princess's foot twice daily for five years. The eventual operation achieved its main objective, though little or nothing could be done at that time to improve the condition of the weak leg itself. The long term effect was that although a slight limp was sometimes noticeable, Princess Marina always wore shoes that were specially designed to correct the imbalance. Throughout her life Marina coped admirably with this minor deformity. As a child she was never known to allow it to impede her games or, for that matter, some of the more strenuous pursuits – swimming, tennis or riding – that she shared with her sisters and their close circle of girl cousins, Helen, later queen of Romania; Irene and Katherine, daughters of Prince Nicholas's elder brother, Constantine, Duke of Sparta, afterwards King Constantine I; and Margarita, Theodora, Cecile and Sophie, daughters of Prince Nicholas's younger brother, Andrew, and older sisters of Prince Philip, Duke of Edinburgh.

In her 1952 study, *The Duchess of Kent,* Jennifer Ellis, one of Marina's earliest biographers, wrote, 'Like all strong-willed, lively children, she was often in conflict with authority. She had ... tremendous force of character. It made her the leader among her sisters and cousins. In her determination not to be left out of anything, she had to take life at a tremendous pace, always trying to catch up with the others, and usually succeeding through sheer will-power. She learnt to swim at three by hurling [herself] into the swimming pool in imitation of Olga's dive. She learnt to ride by galloping off on a horse far too big for her in pursuit of Elizabeth.... She had an invincible courage for any adventure.'

CHAPTER TWO
RUSSIAN TWILIGHT

Princess Marina was already seven by the time her formal education began. Joining her sisters Olga and Elizabeth in their white-walled schoolroom with its view of the Acropolis, she was taught by three governesses. Yet while she learned quickly, particularly in subjects that fired her imagination – literature, geography and art – she lacked concentration in other studies, among them music, mathematics, which always defeated her, and to some extent history. 'You know all the names of the cinema stars,' her exasperated father once admonished her, 'but you don't seem to take the trouble to remember the names of the kings of England.' Whatever her shortcomings may have been in those subjects, Marina made up for them in others. Her aptitude for languages, for instance, meant that as well as Greek and English, in which she had been schooled from birth, she became fluent in French, German, Italian and Russian, the languages that were spoken as a matter of course by her multilingual family.

In art she also excelled, demonstrating particular skill in portraiture, landscape and still life. Many years later, society photographer Cecil Beaton, whose likeness Marina would capture, recalled 'her expression of intense concentration' as, with a dust sheet spread on the floor of her sitting room, 'she worked with crayons and pencils at her easel.' In this her talents mirrored those of her father, who was an accomplished painter in his own right. As a small child Marina would often wander into his studio to watch him at work or dip her fingers into his paints in an attempt to be of assistance. In time, father and daughter would take themselves off, set up their easels and spend long summer afternoons painting side by side. Together they became students of Byzantine religious art and, intrigued by any news they might hear of new archaeological discoveries, frequently accompanied one another to the sites of current excavations.

If interests such as these bound Prince Nicholas and his youngest daughter still closer, they also shared a love of the theatre. Without doubt the cultured and erudite prince was Greece's foremost royal patron of the arts. A poet, a writer and a lover and collector of books, paintings and *objets d'art,* he was also in the privileged position of being able to indulge his passion for drama in the most creative way. For not only did he write and produce a large number of plays, in which he would often appear, but he was able to do so in his very own theatre. In fact, it was on the stage of the Royal Theatre of Greece, which Nicholas would inherit from his father, that the young Princess Marina took part in productions devised by her father; appearing in everything from *tableaux vivants* based on scenes from Greek mythology, to Shakespeare's *The Merchant of Venice* and the famous 17th-century dramatist Pierre Corneille's best-known play, *Le Cid.* Amateur actors, royal or otherwise, were not alone in treading the boards of Prince Nicholas's theatre. On many occasions they were also graced by such august thespians as the legendary Sarah Bernhardt, who, according to contemporary reviews, caused a 'sensation' when she appeared there in *La Dame aux Camélias* in May 1893.

Varied though Marina's life in Athens was, she and her family were at their most content at Tatoi. Among the princess's childhood memories, some of the most vivid were the sounds of the forest, the haunting roar of stags at night; the occasional glimpse of wolves silhouetted against a winter sky; the animals of Tatoi's home farm, where every creature was given a pet name and summer picnics at Phaleron. Nor did time dim the princess's memories of outings to local villages, where residents in national costume ran towards the royal carriages bearing gifts of flowers or embroidery, or of her visits to Spetsai. Though she was never able to explain why, this of all the Greek islands forever remained Marina's favourite.

Inevitably, travel became a prominent feature of the princess's life. To begin with, journeys took the form of holidays, either with her parents and sisters or with Foxy acting as nurse and guardian. Perhaps Marina's earliest journey abroad was that which took place in about 1908, when she, Olga and Elizabeth were taken to Finland to stay with a close friend of Princess Nicholas at her house on the shores of the Gulf. Later, in 1910, Marina was taken to England for the first time. It was then, at the age of three and a half, that she was entertained to tea at Buckingham Palace, and introduced to King George V and Queen Mary who, almost a quarter of a century later, would become her parents-in-law.

In 1910, the year of her husband's accession to the throne, Queen Mary's interest in Marina extended no further than that of a godmother meeting her goddaughter for the first time. During that holiday Prince and Princess Nicholas also took their daughters to Sandringham in Norfolk to visit their great-aunt, the recently widowed Queen Alexandra. Justifiably described as Britain's 'most beautiful queen', 'Aunt Alix', as Prince Nicholas always knew her, had come to Britain from Denmark early in 1863 as the bride of the future King Edward VII, whose death after a 47-year-marriage, she now mourned.

From Sandringham, during that first visit, Marina and her sisters were taken to Bognor. Foxy later recalled, 'Their parents came to see them settled in there, and then HRH Princess Victoria [the second of King Edward VII and Queen Alexandra's three daughters] stayed for some time at the Norfolk Hotel, when she saw a lot of the three little girls, who helped her to bear the sad loss of King Edward, whom, unhappily, Princess Marina never saw.

'At Bognor the Princess and her sisters had a very happy time, and, like less exalted children, busied themselves in making castles and all sorts of fine things in the sand. They were often helped by Princess Victoria and their uncle, Prince Christopher of Greece [known as 'Christo', the youngest of Prince Nicholas's three brothers], who spent some time there.'

Holidays in more exotic locations followed. But in the years before the Revolution, none could quite equal the excitement of family visits to Russia; to Princess Nicholas's mother, Grand Duchess Vladimir (the grand duke himself had died in 1909), and to the family of Prince Nicholas's uncle, Grand Duke Konstantine Konstantinovich, the celebrated playwright and poet known by his initials 'KR', at their palatial houses in St Petersburg and Tsarskoe Selo. Though Marina's personal memories of times spent with her Romanov relations were apparently relatively few – her last visit took place in the summer of 1914, shortly before the outbreak of the First

World War and not long before her eighth birthday – images of people, places and events were sketched in for her, if not by family reminiscences, then by the lessons of history itself.

Among her most distinct memories, however, were the annual journeys she made aboard the imperial train with her parents and sisters. Put at their disposal to ferry them from Sebastopol to St Petersburg every summer – and at the beginning and end of occasional winter visits as well – the train consisted of several carriages, each furnished to afford royal and imperial passengers the greatest possible comfort. The day saloons were richly upholstered, their floors covered with thick carpeting, while the sleeping quarters had proper beds covered with fine linens and eiderdowns of pure silk.

Still greater opulence awaited the family at the Vladimir Palace. Florentine in concept, with rooms – it contained over 300 – designed in a variety of styles, from Neo-Renaissance and Gothic Revival, to Rococo and Oriental, it was the last imperial palace to be built in St Petersburg. Of the mansion on Palace Embankment, Marina's nanny, Miss Fox, wrote to friends back at home, 'Everything is exquisite. My nurseries consist of eight beautifully furnished rooms; dining-room, two saloon ante-rooms, night-nursery, dressing-room, bathroom and so on. There must be a regular army of servants here; it is a huge place. The King's palace in Athens is supposed to be big, but it is nothing like this. We are such a distance from the Grand Duchess's rooms that when I take the children along to their mother I have to wait for them. It is too far to go to fetch them again.'

Astounded though she might have been by the scale and luxury of Grand Duchess Vladimir's way of life, Foxy was not entirely enamoured of the woman herself – 'that majestic personality', as Consuelo Vanderbilt, Duchess of Marlborough, once described her. Foxy's ideas of hygiene did not meet with the grand duchess's approval, and it was to her extreme vexation that, during the Nicholases' first winter visit, she discovered that her granddaughters' nurse insisted on flinging open the carefully fastened windows in the nursery suite. Not one to have the bitter night air wreak havoc with the almost tropical temperature inside the palace, the grand duchess went in person to fasten the windows and put Foxy firmly in her place. No less obstinate than Marie Pavlovna herself, however, Miss Fox immediately reopened the windows the moment the grand duchess's back was turned. From then on the defiant nurse was ever referred to by the grand duchess as 'that dreadful woman'.

Imperious though Grand Duchess Vladimir could be, she was always a doting grandmother, showering gifts of all kinds – toys, dresses, jewellery, even ponies - on Olga, Elizabeth and Marina. A further treat in which the three princesses delighted was when the grand duchess took them into her dressing room to show off her spectacular collection of jewels. Displayed in glass cabinets, there were tiaras and diadems, parures, necklaces, earrings, bracelets and brooches, made up of flawless gems, covering the entire spectrum of precious and semi-precious stones, from diamonds, emeralds and rubies to turquoise, tourmalines and aquamarines, all supplied by famous Russian and French jewellers such as Fabergé, Chaumet and Cartier. Chief among them, however, was a superb tiara of fifteen interlaced diamond circles, each one hung with a drop pearl, which Marie Pavlovna had had made by the Russian court jeweller, Bolin, apparently at the time of her marriage in 1874. Following the grand duchess's death in 1920, a year after she had finally made her escape from revolutionary Russia, Queen Mary bought the 'Vladimir Tiara' as it is known, from Princess Nicholas, who had inherited it from her mother. Today, the tiara is still well known to us as one that is frequently worn by Queen Elizabeth II, to whom it had been bequeathed in 1953, on the death of her grandmother (Queen Mary).

If visits to St Petersburg for the young Greek princesses were tempered, no matter how unintentionally, by an element of formality, the ambience of Grand Duchess Vladimir's palace at Tsarskoe Selo, which the late grand duke had bought in 1875, was more one of leisure and informality. It was here, too, that Princess Marina and her sisters saw much of their uncles, the Grand Duke Kyrill Vladimirovich, eldest of Princess Nicholas's three brothers, and the grand dukes Boris and Andrei. More or less the princesses' own age and, therefore, frequent holiday companions at the nearby Alexander Palace, where they lived with their parents, Tsar Nicholas II and the Empress Alexandra, were the grand duchesses Olga, Tatiana, Maria and Anastasia, and their brother, the Tsarevich Alexey. It was while playing with her second cousins that Marina is believed to have seen the black-robed figure of the so-called Holy Man, Grigori Efimovich Rasputin, 'the mad monk', who would hold unparalleled influence over the tsar and tsarina and their haemophiliac son. Indeed, it is said that Marina watched gravely as Rasputin raised his hand in blessing over the imperial children.

Such then, were Princess Marina's earliest years, set against the backdrop of one of history's most opulent, yet tragically doomed, dynasties. On 28 August 1914, less than a month after Germany had declared war on Russia, the princess, her parents and sisters said farewell to their Romanov relations for what would be the very last time.

CHAPTER THREE

POLITICS AND BATTLESHIPS

The return journey to Greece at the end of that last Russian holiday in 1914 contrasted sharply with the arrival of Prince and Princess Nicholas and their children only a few weeks earlier. Travelling back through Russia, this time aboard a crowded, stuffy train, the family's progress was made even longer and more uncomfortable by repeated delays as their train was halted or shunted into sidings, to permit heavily laden troop trains immediate passage.

In Romania, the Nicholases rested briefly at Pelişor, part of the larger Peleş Castle complex that King Carol had built at Sinaia, in the Carpathian Mountains, before continuing their homeward journey aboard a special train the king put at their disposal. By the time they had crossed from Romania into Serbia, Marina and her sisters, weary and hot, had started to become fractious. 'The heat was unbearable,' Prince Nicholas would later write. 'We had no water and the children cried, until at a railway station we were able to purchase a watermelon with which to quench their thirst.' The discomforts of that particular journey also remained vivid in Marina's memory who, many years later, recalled 'the heat and the flies and the long dreary day, and eventually the watermelon that tasted so good'.

Not so good, however, was the discovery as they reached the frontier between Serbia and Bulgaria that their luggage as well as their servants had disappeared. Exasperated though they were by this turn of events, frayed nerves were calmed by the sight of Marina and her sisters capering around in the diaphanous night-dresses that had been loaned to them by the wife of the local stationmaster. In her 1937 book with the grandiose title, the *Intimate Life Story of HRH The Duchess of Kent – Told for the First Time and Presented with the Personal Approval of Her Royal Highness*, the Russian-born violinist and biographer, Baroness Helena von der Hoven, wrote, 'Those garments were not exactly of the Paris model type, and raised peals of laughter when one of the three sisters simply disappeared in its voluminous folds or tripped over its trailing hem'.

One final stop at Salonika broke the family's long and tedious journey home to Athens. This time, though, the interruption was one of choice rather than necessity. A private pilgrimage, it evoked memories of triumph as well as tragedy. In November 1912 Greece had engaged Turkey, its old and most bitter enemy, in a battle over sovereignty. The campaign itself was brief and at its end the Greek Army, under the command of Prince Nicholas's brother, Crown Prince Constantine had secured a decisive victory which culminated in the seizure of the vital Macedonian port of Salonika or Thessaloniki (Thessalonica) as it is also known.

Freed from the tyrannical rule of their Turkish oppressors, the people celebrated in a frenzy of near-hysteria, welcoming the Greek crown prince as a hero and throwing themselves to the ground in front of his horse. No less jubilant was Constantine's father, King George I. Greatly loved though he was by his people, the king had already announced his intention to abdicate the following year in favour of his eldest son. Although his family attempted to dissuade him, George I was determined to hand his crown to the younger man. 'I shall have reigned for fifty years' he said, 'and it's long enough for any King. I think I'm entitled to a little rest in my old age. Besides, Tino [Crown Prince Constantine's family name] will be able to do far more with the country than I ever could. He was born and bred here, while I am always a foreigner.'

Foreigner or not, the Greek victory at Salonika represented the greatest triumph of King George's entire reign. To honour that achievement, he decided to live there for a time, choosing a house on the shores of the Gulf of Thermai from where he would rule. Few kings could ever have felt more secure in his people's affections than George I, whose arrival in Salonika had been marked by overwhelming demonstrations of loyalty.

Yet, just four months later, on 18 March 1913, the still prevalent air of jubilation was shattered by the king's assassination. Accustomed to walking around the streets of Athens with the same freedom each of his subjects enjoyed, George I thought nothing of doing the same in Salonika, exchanging the time of day with any and all who greeted him. On the afternoon of his death the king accompanied only by his aide-de-camp, Colonel Frankoudis, set out for his usual walk along the waterfront. Two hours or so later, just after five o'clock, as they made their way back, the king and his ADC passed a run-down café from where an anarchist identified as 40-year-old Alexandros Schinas, whom police claimed to be a 'deranged Macedonian', walked up behind him, drew a revolver loaded, according to one contemporary report, with seven bullets and shot the king several times in the back from a range of six feet.

With formal confirmation of the king's death, it fell to Prince Nicholas to summon leading officers of the Greek Army and in 'a voice choked with sobs', as it was described by the press at the time, invited them 'to swear fealty to his brother, the new King Constantine I.

Throughout Europe, King George's royal relations, devastated by the shocking news they received were, like his widowed sister, Queen Alexandra, at home in London, to whom the news had been broken by her daughter Princess Victoria, 'prostrate' with shock and grief.

Young though she was, Princess Marina was no less heartbroken at the loss of her adored grandfather or 'Apapa', as she always called him. And indeed there is a story that when she learned of his death, she flung herself to the floor in an agony of grief. All attempts to console her were apparently to no avail, until Princess Nicholas told her youngest child, who had always been a particular favourite of the late king, 'Apapa wouldn't want you to cry like that. Don't you remember that when you fell down he was always pleased if you were brave?'

Constantine I came to the throne – with his wife Sophie, sister of Germany's Kaiser Wilhem II at his side - earlier than intended and in circumstances none had ever envisaged. In his memoirs, Prince Christopher of Greece would say of his eldest brother, 'No sovereign was ever more popular than Constantine in the early days of his reign. The Greeks, romantic and impressionable, were ready to idolise the soldier

King who had fought side by side with his men, shared camp life with them and led them to victory. He had liberated South Macedonia, Epirus and the Aegean Islands from the Turkish yoke. They began to remember the old legend that Constantinople should be given back to Greece and the Christian Church restored there when a King Constantine and a Queen Sophie reigned in Athens. The tradition probably owed its origins to the fact that the last emperor to fall on the ramparts of Byzantium was named Constantine and his wife was Sophie, but the people had a touching faith in it.'

The visions and hopes the Greeks invested in their new and popular king soared to new heights when, shortly after Constantine and his forces had routed the Turks, they did the same to another of their old foes, the Bulgarians. Both Greece and Bulgaria had long claimed Salonika as their own and in the aftermath of the Greek victory relations between the two countries had been severely strained. Suddenly Bulgarian troops were mobilized; without any formal declaration of war they attacked Salonika. Once more Constantine emerged victorious. 'The welcome he received on his return to Athens was stupendous,' Prince Christopher recalled. 'Thanksgiving services were held in all the churches, crowds besieged the palace, waiting for hours to get a glimpse of him ... The spring and summer of 1914 were the most carefree, the most prosperous Greece had ever known.'

It was in that same carefree spirit that Prince and Princess Nicholas and their daughters had set out for their summer holiday in Russia. But by the end of August, as they broke their homeward journey at Salonika to stand before the memorial that Queen Olga had erected to the memory of her murdered husband, the mood music had changed to a more sombre key. With the start of the Great War, King Constantine, who was known to be something of a Germanophile – he had also undergone military training in Prussia and had married a German princess - vigorously supported a policy of neutrality, despite being pressed by his brother-in-law, Kaiser Wilhelm, to bring Greece into the war on the side of Germany which, together with Austria-Hungary, Bulgaria and the Turks, was fighting against the Triple Entente of Britain, France and Russia. It was the Entente that the Greek Prime Minister, Eleftherious Venizelos, wanted Greece to support militarily. Constantine's refusal to change or modify his political stance set him on a collision course with Venizelos, resulting in the National Schism. With parts of Greece occupied by the Allied forces, and in the hope that support for the Entente would lead to the expansion of Greek territory, Venizelos finally broke ranks and under allied protection, formed a rival administration in Salonika, known as the Provisional Government of National Defence, in direct opposition to the royal government in Athens. Indeed, such were the tensions between the two men that the country was torn by civil war, royalists versus Venizelists.

At the age of ten, Princess Marina knew little or nothing of politics, but as popularity for the royal family ebbed away and the king and his supporters faced increasingly open opposition from the Entente and the Venizelists, one politically motivated incident occurred that she would never forget. In July 1916, in a summer so dry that even the birds in the trees of the parched forest fell silent, arsonists attacked Tatoi with the loss of sixteen lives and the wholesale destruction of forest wildlife. From the house Prince and Princess Nicholas had taken for part of the summer in the foothills of Mount Pentelikon, midway between Athens and Tatoi, Marina, her mother and sisters watched the red glow on the horizon as the royal estate burned.

At Tatoi, King Constantine, his son Paul (the future King Paul I) and estate workers did the best they could to fight the fire until it threatened to surround them. When they could do no more, they made for a goat track that the king hoped would still be passable. Queen Sophie's escape was no less dramatic. Scooping up her three-year-old daughter Katherine, she ran for a mile and a half until, exhausted and terrified, she was picked up by a passing car and driven to the safety of Prince Nicholas's holiday house at Kephisia.

That night, Marina sobbed for the fawns and wild creatures of the forest, and for her 'pet' animals at the home farm. She wept, too, at the thought that her grandfather's tomb might have been destroyed. 'Have they burnt my darling Apapa?' she asked. The answer was no, but when it was time to take stock, less than a quarter of the estate was found to have survived the blaze.

In an ever worsening situation, allied warships blockaded the port of Piraeus and in October, Britain and France frustrated by King

Constantine's unwavering judgement that neutrality was the best policy for Greece, issued an ultimatum. On 2 December, in the belief that
Constantine had finally capitulated, allied troops marched into Athens,
The strength of resistance they encountered forced them to retreat, but
that same afternoon French battleships opened fire and for three hours
relentlessly bombarded the city. As shells exploded near the royal palace,
sending the king and queen together with their household into the cellars
for shelter, Prince Christopher found himself the target of snipers in a
nearby street as he frantically tried to get his car started. 'Mercifully,' he
said later on, 'there were some poor shots in Athens then!'

At the Nicholas Palace, the princesses Marina, Olga and Elizabeth
rushed to the windows of their top-floor nursery from where they
watched the street violence below. It was not until a horrified Princess
Nicholas discovered them transfixed by the bloody scenes of fighting that
the children were hurried to the greater safety of the basement.

Armed confrontation and intense diplomatic negotiations in June
1917 led to the French politician Charles Jonnard, acting in his official
capacity as the Allied Powers' authorized representative, to order the
king's abdication. Though Constantine refused to abdicate, he did agree
to go into exile, taking with him his eldest son Crown Prince George,
whom the Allies considered too pro-German to be trusted. In place of the
ousted king and his rightful heir, the Allies chose Constantine's second
son Alexander as the new occupant of the Greek throne. And it was in
the ballroom of the royal palace on the afternoon of 11 June 1917, with
tears in his eyes and his voice breaking with emotion, that the 23-year-old
prince swore the oath of loyalty to the Greek constitution. It was an event
devoid of all ceremony and attended only by the Archbishop of Athens,
who administered the oath, the king's Prime Minister, Alexandros Zaimis,
and Alexander's father and elder brother. Afterwards, Constantine told
the new King Alexander I that as a puppet king he should regard himself
as regent, rather than true monarch. 'His crown,' said his uncle, Prince
Christopher, 'was a mockery, but he wore it with dignity.'

Entirely alone, the young king, who was to occupy the throne until his
shocking death little more than three years later, was kept under constant
surveillance. His household was chosen for him and any so-called 'courtiers'

who became too friendly were summarily dismissed. Yet perhaps the cruellest deprivation of all for Alexander was the complete loss of communication with his family. Even as he lay dying, something we will come to shortly, his distracted mother Queen Sophie was not permitted at his bedside.

In the second week of June 1917, however, two days after Alexander I had assumed the role of monarch, his family set sail for life as exiles. Yet, at Oropos on the Gulf of Euboea, in highly emotional scenes, loyal supporters massed on the landing stage and on the beach, wailing like 'bewildered children', attempted to prevent the royal family's departure. As Prince Nicholas would recall, 'The nearer the King and Queen drew to [their] boat, the fiercer grew the frenzy of the people who tried to keep [King Constantine] back by force. Many leapt into the sea and held fast to the boat ... Among the lamentations and sobs that rent the air the boat set slowly off, whilst all the people went down on their knees and stretched out their hands towards the King and Queen. It was a heartrending picture.'

Describing the uneasy mood in Athens, Prince Christopher later wrote, '... the once gay little capital was like the city of the dead. No one went out in the streets, all the theatres and shops were closed. Those of us of the royal family who remained behind lived in an atmosphere of suspicion. Everyone known to have been faithful to King Constantine was put under arrest. Men and women in all walks of life – statesmen, lawyers, writers, officers of both Army and Navy – were mysteriously denounced, hauled before a tribunal and sentenced, some to years of imprisonment, others to banishment in remote islands.'

With the sole exception of King Alexander, banishment was also the fate of the entire Greek royal family. On 4 July 1917, Princess Marina and her family, together with Prince Christopher, and followed by Prince and Princess Andrew (Prince Nicholas's brother and sister-in-law, the former Princess Alice of Battenberg) and their four daughters, sailed away from Athens at the start of their first journey into exile. Initially short of money and reliant on the generosity of loyal friends, the royal party made tracks to Switzerland. There for the next three years, the exiled royals divided their time between Zurich and Lucerne, where they spent their summers, and St Moritz, where they lived in winter.

Prince and Princess Nicholas felt the deprivations of exile more keenly than their daughters. With the adaptability of youth Marina, then aged eleven and Olga and Elizabeth, aged fourteen and thirteen respectively, regarded Switzerland as a new adventure and, despite occasional pangs of homesickness, soon became acclimatized to their surroundings. For Marina with her nascent talent as a watercolourist, Switzerland was an inspiration. Under the tutelage of a professional art teacher, she was soon interpreting the beauty of the countryside through the medium of her paint box. No less diverting was the awakening of new interests. Among them, in due season, were winter sports including skiing, skating and tobogganing.

For Marina's parents, uncles and aunts, however, Switzerland was not so great an adventure. Despite the relative tranquillity of the country surrounded as it was by the maelstrom of war, the Greek royal family was still regarded with the deepest suspicion. 'Here in the calm and peacefulness of this neutral country,' Prince Nicholas later wrote, 'we were still marked down as dangerous, political intriguers who had to be closely watched, and shunned by everyone belonging to the Entente nations.' As if passive hostility were not enough, the family suffered humiliation in other ways. They were not allowed to leave the country; friends could only visit under conditions of strict secrecy; and their mail, though perhaps unsurprisingly, was invariably censored. Even Kate Fox, the princesses' nurse, was not exempt from the controlling influence of Greece's ruling regime. Summoned to the British Consul, she was warned that unless she resigned her position with the 'traitors', as the family was described, and returned immediately to England, her passport would be confiscated. Outraged, but faced with little choice, she told the family as she prepared to leave, that she would come back to them, and when peace did finally return, she kept that promise.

Uncomfortable though exile was for them, Prince and Princess Nicholas faced up to it with admirable stoicism. Yet even so, most of the claims made in later years by the more romantically minded that the family experienced nothing but hardship and penury are not supported by hard fact. Poverty is of course relative and when compared to the wealth and privilege they enjoyed at home when the going was good (and would be again), the Nicholases did find themselves obliged to live within their means, keeping a careful eye on expenditure and seldom indulging in anything that might be considered unnecessary or a luxury. In practical terms, Prince Nicholas also decided to utilize his skills as a painter to help supplement his family's resources. Of the opinion that he painted 'at least as well as Mr Winston Churchill' (Britain's future and most celebrated Prime Minister was also a gifted amateur painter) Prince Nicholas rented an artist's studio in the Montreux suburb of Territet. Before long, under the pseudonym 'Nicholas le Prince', he staged his first exhibition. His paintings not only sold well on that occasion, but continued to do so afterwards. In time, Princess Marina who as we saw earlier often joined her father on his painting trips at home in Greece, would find her own work – including watercolour portraits of her sisters, her daughter Alexandra, and her niece Princess Margaret – displayed in public exhibitions or occasionally published in magazines such as *Vogue*.

Professional soldier, painter and even playwright though Prince Nicholas might have been, he was above all a family man and at home Sundays had always been set aside for informal family gatherings at the royal palace. In exile, the royal family continued to see much of one another though concern for the young King Alexander, isolated in Athens, meant that get-togethers were sometimes rather melancholy affairs. For Prince and Princess Nicholas, there was also anxiety about their respective mothers, the dowager Queen Olga and Grand Duchess Vladimir. At the start of the Great War, both women – one a Russian grand duchess by birth, the other by marriage – had, like other members of the imperial family, established military hospitals, Queen Olga's at the family estate at Pavlovsk, not far from Tsarskoe Selo, and Grand Duchess Vladimir's at Kislovodsk, a fashionable spa town in the North Caucasus. With the outbreak of Revolution, both women found themselves dangerously cut off, even though Prince Christopher, as he put it, hoped his mother, Olga, 'would be perfectly safe among the people who had known her since childhood'.

With members of the imperial family being taken captive by the Bolsheviks and brutally murdered, it was a vain hope. As it turned out, delicate and strenuous diplomacy on the part of the Danish Embassy in

St Petersburg, or Petrograd as it had now become, resulted in Queen Olga being able to leave Russia and in July 1918, was finally reunited with her family. In his memoirs, Prince Christopher recalled, 'My mother was only the ghost of her old self when she joined us in Switzerland. The months of worry and suspense and the privations she had undergone had worn her to skin and bone. The events in Greece had tortured her with anxiety, far away from us all as she was and unable even to get accurate news; and in addition she had had the grief of losing seventeen members of her family [among them three of her nephews, the princes Ioann, Konstantin and Igor Konstantinovich, Tsar Nicholas and Empress Alexandra and their five children, Grand Duke Michael Alexandrovich, the tsar's younger brother, and Grand Duchess Elisabeth Feodorovna, the tsarina's sister who in her widowhood had established and become Abbess of the nursing order and community of Saints Martha and Mary in Moscow] in the Russian Revolution.... Like everyone else who came out of Russia she was half starved, for a diet of bread soaked in oil ... is not exactly nourishing and it was some time before she recovered her health.'

Traumatic though Queen Olga's experiences had been, it was not until February 1920 that Grand Duchess Vladimir, who held the dubious distinction of having been the last of the Romanovs to do so, was able to get out of Russia. Before escaping aboard a fishing boat to Anapa, an ancient town on the northern coast of the Black Sea, Marie Pavlovna's house in Kislovodsk was said to have been searched by revolutionaries on no fewer than twenty-two occasions. Having spent fourteen months in Anapa, the grand duchess who had refused earlier opportunities to escape (via Constantinople) lest she should be subjected to the indignity of being deloused, finally agreed to go when the White Russian commander, General Wrangel, told her that he could no longer guarantee her safety.

Without further protest, Grand Duchess Vladimir, that grandest of grand duchesses, set out on what would be an uncomfortable seven week journey to the port of Novorossiysk. There, purely by chance, she met another imperial escapee, her husband's niece Grand Duchess Olga Alexandrovna, sister of Nicholas II, who on a journey that would take her via Istanbul and Belgrade eventually reached Denmark where she joined her mother, the dowager empress. Of that meeting, as Ian Vorres wrote in his 1965 biography *The Last Grand Duchess,* Olga would recall, 'Disregarding peril and hardship, [Marie Pavlovna] stubbornly kept to all the trimmings of bygone splendour and glory. And somehow she carried it off... When even generals found themselves lucky to find a horse cart and an old nag to bring them to safety, Aunt Miechen made a long journey in her own train. It was battered all right -- but it was hers.'

On 13 February 1920, Grand Duchess Vladimir finally embarked on an Italian ship bound for Venice. From there, travelling via Paris, she made her way to Switzerland. Like Queen Olga, the indomitable Marie Pavlovna stepped down from her train the shadow of her former self. At the age of sixty-six, white-haired and thinner than her family could remember ever having seen her, she was completely worn out by her long ordeal. For several weeks she enjoyed the company of Nicholas, Ellen and her three granddaughters before travelling on to Contrexvéille, a famous health resort in north-east France, where she hoped to recover her health. Instead, it deteriorated and only two months later, on 6 September, Grand Duchess Vladimir died. Sudden, perhaps even tragic, though her death was, in Greece at that time a far more tragic incident was about to claim a life which, in many ways, had hardly begun.

Chapter Four
A BRIEF RETURN

One month after the death of Grand Duchess Vladimir news reached the exiled royal family that King Alexander lay dying at Tatoi. In shocked disbelief, they heard how on 2 October the 27-year-old king had spent part of the day working on his motorbike. Without changing out of his greasy overalls he had then taken Fritz, his German shepherd dog, for a walk. On his way back he called in on the keeper of the estate's vineyards and his wife. It was while talking with them that one of the keeper's pet Barbary macaques attacked or had been attacked by Fritz. In attempting to separate them a second monkey attacked the king, inflicting two bites to his arm and ankle. Despite the wounds having been cleaned and dressed, they became infected and septicaemia set in.

From Switzerland, the king's desperate mother, Queen Sophie, begged repeatedly to be allowed to return to Greece to be with her son who in his delirium on 19 October, had been calling out for her. When the Greek government refused the queen's pleas she asked, in utter despair, if her mother-in-law Queen Olga might be allowed to travel to Athens to be with her grandson. This request was granted, but delayed by rough seas the dowager queen's arrival at Tatoi came too late. King Alexander had died twelve hours earlier at 5.20pm on 25 October 1920.

In a sense, the monkey bites that led to the unexpected death of Greece's puppet king also claimed a second victim. For in permitting Queen Olga's return, Prime Minister Venizelos underestimated the wealth of popular feeling that surrounded the widow of the nation's much loved King George I. In the general election of 15 November that had been called before Alexander's death, Venizelos was defeated. Of the 370 seats in the Greek parliament, his party had won only 120. Amid scenes of rejoicing, the new 'royalist' Prime Minister, Dimitrios Rallis, asked to see the queen dowager. When she received him, Rallis was so overcome with emotion as he knelt to kiss Queen Olga's hand that she had to urge him to rise. When he refused, she too went down on her knees, assuring him that she would not get up unless he did. The purpose of Rallis' emotional mission was to ask the queen to become regent of Greece, pending the return of the rightful sovereign, King Constantine I. It was an office she held until her son returned to the throne on 19 December, following the plebiscite he had personally called for to gauge the nation's wishes. Of the 1,010,788 votes cast, only 10,883 were opposed to the king's return.

The reception King Constantine and Queen Sophie received when they arrived in Athens was euphoric. Prince Nicholas, who had already seized the moment and returned home to the Nicholas Palace with Ellen, Marina, Olga and Elizabeth, described the scene, 'The royal train had been shunted on to a side-line which, running through one of the streets, ended at a small square, where we awaited its arrival. When they saw it coming about a mile off, the people could not contain their emotion. The cry *Erchetai! Erchetai!* ('He is coming! He is coming!') – which had been the password ever since they heard that the King was on his way to Greece – rose like the roar of an ocean wave. The engine, all beflagged, was painfully ploughing its way through a seething mass of people yelling, crying, gesticulating, sobbing hysterically .... Slowly the train crawled to its destination, and came to a halt in front of where our mother stood. She stepped first into the carriage, and we followed her to greet the King. It would be impossible to describe his emotion; imagine what deep sorrows he had been through, and what this spontaneous manifestation of loyalty and love from his people meant to him!'

In the midst of the scenes Prince Nicholas went on to describe at even greater length, few could have guessed that the royal family's joyful return to Greece would be short lived. On the horizon yet more storm clouds – a legacy of the Venizelist years – that were already gathering would bring with them another and still longer exile for the Greek royals. For the moment, however, Princess Marina was able to celebrate her fourteenth birthday on 13 December with a proper family celebration at home in Athens. On the threshold of young adulthood, Marina was now a tall, slender girl with rich brown hair framing a clear-skinned oval face. Indeed, her striking good looks had already started to turn heads. Friends of her parents frequently remarked upon Marina's high cheekbones and amber-coloured eyes, while her somewhat crooked smile was described by admirers as 'enchanting'. In later years her voice – to some fascinating, to others guttural and unbecoming – was both deep and husky. Her speech was clipped and staccato, and her accent, sometimes described as 'slightly Greek', was as Russian as her mother's.

For Princess Marina and her family, another cause for celebration at this time was the return of their beloved 'Foxy' in the capacity of loyal retainer, which somehow seemed to strengthen the growing sense of normality in Athens generally and, indeed, at the palace of Tatoi, which had recently been rebuilt. For Marina, however, the return to normality also meant a return to the schoolroom, though that unwelcome routine was often outweighed by more pleasurable diversions; among them on 10 March 1921, for instance, was the wedding of Marina's cousin Princess Helen – or 'Sitta' as she was known – the eldest of King Constantine's three daughters to Crown Prince Carol of Romania, afterwards King Carol II. In Corfu, exactly three months later, on 10 June, Marina's aunt Alice, Princess Andrew of Greece – having already had four daughters - gave birth to a son who was registered under the name of Philippos. Then sixth in line to the Greek throne he would, twenty-six years later, marry Britain's future Queen Elizabeth II no longer as Prince Philippos of Greece and Denmark, but as Lieutenant Philip Mountbatten RN, newly-created His Royal Highness The Duke of Edinburgh.

It was also at about this time that Princess Marina's lifelong friendship with Princess Juliana of the Netherlands (later Queen Juliana, who reigned from 1948 until her abdication in 1980) first began. Juliana, who was three years younger than Marina, had recently developed an interest in philately and to acquire Greek stamps for her collection, her mother, Queen Wilhelmina, suggested that Juliana should write to the youngest of Prince Nicholas's daughters. In time the rapport the two princesses established as penfriends developed into a warm personal friendship. As they grew up they often visited one another and when, in 1934, Princess Marina married, Juliana was one of her bridesmaids. Later still, during the

1960s, Marina was among the special guests at the celebrations of Queen Juliana's and her husband Prince Bernhard's silver wedding anniversary.

But to return to the years of Marina's youth, and it was apparent that through her burgeoning sophistication and sense of self worth, she would become every bit as aware of her royal and imperial heritage as her mother. However, it did nothing to diminish her sense of humour or her enthusiasm for enjoying life. Baroness Helena von der Hoven cites one example of the simple games Marina and some of her cousins enjoyed playing on an island adjoining Spetsai. Called 'Keeping House', it centred on a favourite fig tree.

'One crossed in a sailing boat to this island and picnicked on the beach,' the baroness wrote. 'Then one climbed the tree. Each member of the party had her own branch which represented her 'room' and all the figs on this branch were entirely her property. One could visit each other and exchange fruit which was carefully passed over on fresh green leaves. It needed a lot of agility not to drop any and if such a misfortune happened it was greeted with a lot of merry laughter and jokes.

'Though one of the youngest, Princess Marina was always the ringleader and kept the company in fits of laughter by mimicking her governess of whom she gave striking imitations. There were also other pranks which necessitated a certain amount of tactics and daring, and her contemporaries learned to know so well that humorous, half-wistful, half-mischievous smile of the young Princess Marina.

'One of the favourite games in those days was shooting arrows. The bows were home-made out of flexible branches tied firmly with a bit of string and great competition took place as to who should produce the best weapon. It was great fun hiding behind trees and rocks and shooting at invisible enemies, and Robin Hood and other similar heroes were very popular at that time.'

Away from the realms of make-believe there were few heroes in the Greece of the early 1920s for Princess Marina, her sisters and cousins to look up to or emulate. In January 1921, though much against the king's wishes, Greek forces had again been mobilized to take on the Turks, this time over the question of sovereignty in Asia Minor. Prosecuted until September 1922, the war resulted in the wholesale slaughter of much of the Greek army. Over 300,000 troops, including King Constantine and his brothers Nicholas and Andrew, had gone to war marching, as Prince Christopher put it, 'straight into the wasps' nest prepared by that military genius, Mustafa Kemal'.

Inevitably someone had to take responsibility for the decimation of Greek forces at Smyrna, and that someone, conveniently, perhaps obviously, was King Constantine himself. In the meantime with her husband away at war, and Marina on what was to be an extended visit to England with Miss Fox, Princess Nicholas accepted an invitation to stay in Cannes with her brother-in-law Prince Christopher and his immensely rich American wife, the twice-widowed Nonie (otherwise Nancy) Stewart Worthington Leeds or 'the Dollar Princess', as the one-time stenographer was known in the United States.

Olga and Elizabeth accompanied Princess Nicholas to Cannes and it was there in the spring of 1922 that Olga met and became engaged to her distant cousin Crown Prince Frederick of Denmark, the twenty-three-year-old son of King Christian X. At that time, Olga was arguably the most physically attractive of Prince and Princess Nicholas's daughters and before long she was being enthusiastically, if fatuously, described in the popular press as 'the most beautiful princess in Europe'. Nevertheless, Crown Prince Frederick, or 'Rico', as he was known in family circles, was greatly enamoured and attentively 'paid court', as it was then called, to the young princess. For her part, Olga was completely overwhelmed by the speed at which she was being wooed and apparently won, for, as Neil Balfour – her future son-in-law – explained in his biography *Paul of Yugoslavia,* 'She was just nineteen and though in behaviour and manner well trained and therefore seemingly grown up and sophisticated, she was at heart a child, romantic and vulnerable ... a pious teenager, conscious of her role as the eldest daughter and longing to think "the right thoughts" and feel "the right feelings".

As the weeks slipped by, however, and hopes for a late summer wedding began to fade, so it started to become painfully obvious that Prince Frederick's ardour was beginning to cool. Then, suddenly, as Prince Christopher put it, 'a misunderstanding arose'. That 'misunderstanding', as friends of Princess Marina later assessed it, had a lot to do with Frederick's fondness for the bottle. Indeed, it has been said that when Rico and Olga appeared in public on one occasion, the prince was so completely drunk that, instead of taking Olga's hand in his own to acknowledge the cheers of the small crowd, he took that of her sister Elizabeth instead. It isn't certain whether that one incident constituted the sudden 'misunderstanding' Prince Christopher referred to, but very clearly something had occurred to cause a rift between the couple. That September Rico and Olga agreed to meet in order to discuss the future. On 8 September the bewildered princess, who might have become queen of Denmark, confided to her diary, 'If only I knew what a state of mind he is in! Is he still bitter and resolved to break off the engagement? I only hope he will listen to me and after that if he still remains the same it means he never really loved me!' Three days later Rico and Olga talked together for almost an hour, but, wrote the princess, '.. he had quite made up his mind to give it up. I said I was willing to try again but he said he had no more love for me (it couldn't have been very strong while it was there).'

Distressing though the whole sorry episode had undoubtedly been for both the Greek and Danish royal families, it can't be said that Princess Olga had lost her ideal husband. Neil Balfour wrote, 'The pressure was certainly there for the engagement to continue, and although Olga had tried to steel herself for the occasion, she was inevitably apprehensive. She had scarcely had time to fall in love with Rico, but she had enjoyed the flattery and attention and had responded in all the established ways. She had subsequently realized that her dreams of a romantic love affair ... ending happily ever after in marriage were an illusion'.

At a family gathering soon after Olga's engagement had officially ended, the 'marital' post-mortem was interrupted by the sixteen-year-old Princess Marina. Sitting quietly sketching by a window, she had all but been forgotten by the adults locked in earnest discussion until a voice demanded, 'Why the hell should Olga marry him if she doesn't love him! I wouldn't.' Princess Nicholas turned to Prince Christopher and smiled: 'Out of the mouths of babes ...' One year later, Olga did marry for love; but a further thirteen years were to pass before Crown Prince Frederick, later King Frederick IX of Denmark, took a wife and when he did, in May 1935, his bride was Princess Ingrid of Sweden, the only daughter of Britain's Princess Margaret of Connaught and her husband the Swedish crown prince, afterwards King Gustav VI Adolf.

Marina's visit to England during the spring and early summer of 1922 meant that she missed the initial excitement of her sister's ill-starred engagement. But, when she and Foxy arrived in London, there was more than enough family news to catch up on. Visiting George V and Queen Mary at Windsor and Queen Alexandra at Sandringham, for instance, meant hearing all about the wedding that February of the king and queen's only daughter, Princess Mary to Henry, Viscount Lascelles, later Earl of Harewood; and through letters and postcards, following the progress of Edward, Prince of Wales, known as 'David' to his family, who was then on official tour of the Far East.

For Marina, indeed for her entire family, the freedom to travel after the restricted years in Switzerland was both a pleasure and a relief. But to travel through choice was one thing; to wander as an exile quite another. The disastrous campaign in Asia Minor concluded that September meant that when Marina rejoined her family, she did so as a refugee once more. In 1922 Greece had demanded – and this time secured – the formal abdication of King Constantine. Then, as before, those in power expelled all but two members of the royal family: Prince George, who now became King George II and Constantine's brother, Prince Andrew.

Taking revenge against those considered to have been responsible for the war, disillusioned army officers arrested several prominent ministers. Shortly afterwards Prince Andrew, now back at home at his villa Mon Repos on the island of Corfu, was requested to travel to Athens in order to give evidence at their trial. No sooner had he arrived than he himself was arrested and imprisoned, accused of having helped instigate the war with Turkey.

Among his family – now in Italy at the start of their second exile – concern for Prince Andrew was exacerbated by the fact that all communication with him was forbidden. His guards, as his brother Christopher recalled, 'kept the strictest watch and confiscated all letters and parcels .... Even food sent in by sympathizers was closely examined and a *foie gras* in aspic, with which a dear old lady intended to console him, was hacked to pieces before he was allowed to eat it.' Finally, in a desperate attempt to make contact with the prisoner, Prince Christopher 'hit on the happy expedient of writing a letter on cigarette paper, rolling it tightly and putting it with other cigarettes into his valet's case. In this way it reached him safely. He answered it with a short note full of courage, but reading between the lines I knew that he had no longer any hope of regaining his freedom. He had just had a conversation with his former school friend, M. Pangalos, now Minister of War, and instigator of his trial, that had left him small grounds for optimism.

'How many children have you?' Pangalos had asked suddenly and, when my brother, surprised at the irrelevance of the question, told him he shook his head: "Poor things, what a pity they will soon be orphans!".

Each of the imprisoned ministers charged with high treason, for having 'voluntarily and by design permitted the incursion of foreign troops into the territory of the Kingdom' faced the firing squad. The same fate, however, despite his apparently doom-laden exchange with the new Minister of War, did not await Prince Andrew. For while the court martial found him guilty of disobeying an order during a battle and abandoning his post in the face of the enemy, he escaped sentence of death due, as it was officially put, to his 'lack of experience in commanding a large unit'. Instead, he was sentenced to 'degradation of rank and banishment [from Greece] for life.' Behind the scenes, pressure had also been mounting after the prince's family made effective representations to powerful people. Princess Andrew dispatched appeals to several European heads of state; Queen Olga wrote to the kings of England and Spain; while Princess Christopher (or Princess Anastasia as Nonie/Nancy was now known) appealed to the pope. All had reacted positively, urgently sending emissaries to Athens. But it was the government of Andrew's British cousin King George V that sent HMS *Calypso*, a C-class light cruiser that had seen action during the Second Battle of Heligoland Bight in 1917, to Phaleron to effect the prince's highly-secret departure on the afternoon of 3 December 1922. Already on board was Andrew's wife Princess Alice. Next day, *en route* to southern Italy from where, via Brindisi, Rome and Paris, the family made its way to London, the *Calypso* paused briefly at Corfu to pick up Andrew and Alice's five children, the youngest of whom was the eighteen-month-old Prince Philip.

Towards the end of what had been a profoundly disturbing year Princess Nicholas, who had only recently recovered from diphtheria, left

Paris – where she had stayed since the end of Olga's engagement – for Palermo. In the Sicilian capital, where members of the royal family had gathered, she re-joined her husband, and the now ex-King Constantine and Queen Sophie. When Princess Marina and her sister Elizabeth also arrived after a short holiday in Chamonix, Marina immediately summed up the general sense of dismay by saying – though not without a touch of humour – 'We really needn't have unpacked our trunks.' For the next year or so Prince Nicholas and his family would find themselves packing and unpacking with increased regularity, until they eventually settled on somewhere to live. Their travels had already begun in a small way after they grew restless in Palermo (where King Constantine was to die of a stroke at the age of fifty-four, in January 1923) and moved on to what Princess Olga, until recently surrounded by the gilded splendour of the Ritz in Paris, unhappily described as a 'Godforsaken ... perfectly foul' hill-top hotel in San Remo. Nevertheless, it was there in circumstances distinctly at odds with what they had been used to, that Prince and Princess Nicholas and their daughters spent the Christmas of 1922.

Early in the New Year, they were on the move once again, this time to Merano in the Tyrol, where both Marina and Elizabeth underwent operations for the removal of their adenoids. As they recuperated, their parents took Olga to Florence, where, to her delight, they spent three absorbing weeks visiting the palaces, museums and art galleries Prince Nicholas had so often spoken of. By the beginning of April, the family was making plans to visit England; an idea suggested to them by George V's sister Princess Victoria, otherwise Cousin 'Toria', with a view to their doing 'the Season', and perhaps hoping that Olga might attract the attention of the Prince of Wales, *the* most eligible royal bachelor in the world. Leaving Merano on 31 May, the family booked into the Granby Court Hotel in Queen's Gate, Kensington eight days later.

CHAPTER FIVE
PARISIAN EXILE

For Prince and Princess Nicholas, as for their elder daughters Olga and Elizabeth, the summer season of 1923 was a non-stop round of social engagements. There were lunches and dinners at Buckingham Palace, Claridge's, and the famous Embassy Club. There were balls hosted by Lady Zia Wernher (daughter of Tsar Nicholas I's grandson Grand Duke Mikhail Mikhailovich and his morganatic wife, Countess Sophie de Torby), the Duchess of Sutherland, Sir Philip Sassoon, the Duchess of Portland, and the Red Cross. There were sporting fixtures such as the Wimbledon Tennis championships, the Royal Horse Show, and polo matches at Roehampton, Ranelagh and Hurlingham, and there were tea- and cocktail-parties, theatre visits and a royal garden party at Buckingham Palace. Despite their apparently modest means, they also made forays to the most fashionable of London's shops and stores.

For Princess Olga there was also romance though not with the heir to the British throne. At Lady Zia Wernher's ball, Prince Paul of Yugoslavia saw the twenty-year-old Olga quite literally across a crowded room and although they were not even introduced that night, fell in love with her. So smitten was he that he contrived to get himself invited to all the functions Olga was most likely to attend. On 10 July, Paul achieved his objective, but appeared to make no great impression. At subsequent events he was infinitely more successful; so much so, that by the 29th of that month, when they went to the cinema together, it is said Olga sensed the reason for Paul's nervousness and, when he proposed, she immediately accepted.

Prince Paul of Serbia, as he was then known, had been born in St Petersburg in April 1893, the only child of Prince Arsène Karageorgevich of Serbia and Countess Aurora Pavlovna Demidova. A nephew of King

Peter I of Serbia, Paul, who would act as Regent of Yugoslavia from 1934 to 1941, during the minority of King Peter II, was educated in Switzerland and at Christ Church, Oxford. As an undergraduate he lived in considerable style, employing two servants as well as a chauffeur to drive his Daimler limousine. Later, when he came down, he took a flat in Mount Street, Mayfair, which he shared with fellow man about town Prince Serge Obolensky. A colourful character whose four wives would include Ekaterina Alexandrovna, the natural daughter of Tsar Alexander II by his mistress and later second wife, Ekaterina Dolgorukova, and Ava, daughter of John Jacob Astor IV, Obolensky would eventually become a lieutenant-colonel in the U.S. paratroopers and later still, vice-chairman of the Board of Hilton Hotels.

But to return to Prince Paul and in spite of his background and unquestionable loyalty to Yugoslavia, he was very much an anglophile. Not only was his outlook decidedly British, but so too were the majority of his closest friends, among them 'Bertie' and Elizabeth, the Duke and Duchess of York, who in 1936 were to become King George VI and Queen Elizabeth.

With Olga taking centre stage during this particular family visit, the sixteen-year-old Princess Marina's own diary looked decidedly unexciting. Watching the Royal Tournament, for example, even if it was from the royal box, hardly matched up to the glamour of an event like the Duchess of Sutherland's fancy-dress masked ball at Hampden House in Green Street, Mayfair, to which the Prince of Wales and his brother 'Bertie', Duke of York, in homage it was said to Oscar Asche's popular musical comedy, *Chu Chin Chow*, arrived dressed as Chinese coolies. Having got wind of their intention, their hostess also wore oriental costume and other guests followed her example.

Too young and still not 'out' as a 'debutante' to take part in any of it herself, Marina watched from the wings as high society performed its annual summer ritual. A few months later, however, she and her sister Elizabeth, were very much part of the celebrations when, on 22 October, Olga and Paul were married in the chapel of the Old Palace in Belgrade. Before the ceremony, conducted according to the rites of the Greek Orthodox Church, 'Puppy' and 'Mummy', as Olga called her parents, blessed the bride with a holy icon. Then at midday the Minister of the Court arrived to lead Olga, wearing a slender, draped white satin wedding dress and lace veil, and her father in procession through the palace to the candle-lit chapel. At the altar Prince Paul, dressed in his be-medalled ceremonial uniform, plumed helmet and high boots, waited with his best man, the Duke of York. Among the congregation, in places of honour, sat Paul's cousin King Alexander of Serbia and his wife Marie, King Ferdinand and Queen Marie of Romania, the Serbian monarch's in-laws, and the Duchess of York. Also present was Queen Elisabeth of Greece, wife of Princess Olga's uncle King George II and herself the eldest daughter of the Romanian king and his flamboyant consort.

Olga and Paul's wedding would mark the end of a relatively settled period in the lives of the Greek royal family, for only two months later, in December 1923, Greece was declared a republic and like the rest of their relations George II and Queen Elisabeth faced exile. Over the next twelve years, during which George II and his queen increasingly grew apart, he spending much of his time in London, she in Romania, Greece would see twenty-three changes of government, a dictatorship and thirteen coups before the country's 'part-time' monarchy was once again restored in November 1935. When the royal family returned once more, however, Queen Elisabeth was not among them. Her unhappy experiences in Greece, as one of her visitors, the American Professor George Huntington, put it, had 'darkened the face of the world for her'. In July that year, when restoration of the monarchy was on the cards, King George and Queen Elisabeth were divorced. Returning to her native land, Elisabeth reclaimed Romanian nationality which she had had to surrender at the time of her marriage, and lived a more contented life on an estate of her own in western Romania, in a palace she had built in Bucharest and later at a villa in Cannes where she died in 1956, once again an exile following the communist takeover of Romania.

In the meantime, events in the life of her former husband, King George II, were to be as turbulent as ever. In April 1941, just five years after his return, the German invasion of Greece during the Second World War forced him out of the country yet again, only to be restored to the throne as the result of a plebiscite in September 1946. Seven months later, on 1 April, at the age of only fifty-six he died suddenly of arteriosclerosis. George was succeeded by his only surviving brother Paul, who is said to have remarked on his accession that 'the most important tool for a King of Greece is a suitcase.' Unlike his predecessors, King Paul I, who would reign for seventeen years until his untimely death in March 1964, never needed a suitcase. But his son who succeeded him as King Constantine II certainly did. Just three years into his reign and three years after he had married Princess Anne-Marie of Denmark, youngest daughter of the very same King Frederick, or 'Rico', who, as crown prince had once been fleetingly engaged to Princess Marina's sister Olga, the young king and his family were forced to flee the country in the teeth of a military coup. Six years later, in 1973, following the restoration of democracy, a referendum opposed Constantine's return.

In 1923, however, all these events lay in the unknowable future as Princess Olga and Prince Paul set off on their honeymoon which they spent in Venice, Florence and Rome; and Prince and Princess Nicholas with Marina and Elizabeth returned to Paris. Between leaving London at the end of the 1923 'Season' and their visit to Belgrade that October, the family had stayed briefly at the Campbell Hotel on the fashionable Avenue Friedland. But when Greece again became a republic, Prince and Princess Nicholas took the decision to make Paris their home. For a while they rented a furnished service flat near the Trocadero, but then found a much larger, better appointed unfurnished apartment on the Boulevard Jules Sandeau, near Porte de la Muette on the edge of the Bois de Boulogne.

It was at around this time, in fact, although he was by no means poor nor anywhere near the bread line, that Prince Nicholas, shrewdly recognizing an opportunity to gain financially from the misfortune of exile, entered into negotiations with the owners of the Grand Bretagne, at that time Athens' leading hotel and today still considered to be one of the most luxurious in southern Europe. In anticipation of their interest, Nicholas offered the hotel's owners a lease on his own palace in the city in return for an appreciable income that would do much to support his family's lifestyle during their enforced absence. Within weeks a deal had been agreed and the Nicholas Palace, renamed Le Petit Palais, became a suitably royal annex to the Grand Bretagne. The arrangement also meant that Prince

Nicholas was able to recover some of the family's furniture and *objets*. Shipped to France and installed in their new apartment, they created a pleasing air of familiarity in their fresh surroundings. As soon as they moved in, Marina and Elizabeth selected their own bedrooms and to their delight were also given a separate sitting room in which to entertain their friends and cousins, without having to disturb their parents in the rooms they had chosen.

Before long, in order to give form to his days, Prince Nicholas who would ruefully say, 'To be born a prince is an accident, but not always a privilege and by no means a career', took up his paintbrush once again and once again the work of 'Nicholas le Prince' began appearing in the art galleries of Paris. Once again Princess Marina's father was flattered by the number of commissions that came his way accompanied, naturally, by the appropriate fees. As one observer put it, Prince Nicholas was, 'far more in his own element in the studios of the Left Bank and in the society of artists, writers and musicians, than in the round of official engagements which had filled his days in Athens.' Similarly, it was also said that Princess Marina 'loved this Paris of the artist. Ever since her childhood in Athens, when she had run into her father's studio and coaxed him into letting her use his paints, they shared an absorbing interest in art. Through their adventures, even when her other lessons had been neglected, he had seen that she studied under the best teachers.'

Despite being more mature than many girls fast approaching the age of seventeen – and in those days young people were not nearly as street-wise or switched on as they are today – the disruptive influence of Greek politics meant that Marina's formal education was not as complete as her mother would have wished. To remedy the situation, Princess Nicholas decided that a year at finishing school would benefit her youngest daughter. The school the princess chose at Auteuil not only recommended itself because it catered for the individual requirements of girls of every nationality, but also because it was run by a family friend, the Russian Princess Vera Mestchersky. Marina herself was far from enthusiastic at the prospect of leaving home, and the thought of regulated hours and strict discipline made her thoroughly miserable. But as her mother had presented her with a *fait accompli*, she had little choice but to grit her teeth and get on with it.

'At first we didn't understand her,' said one former school friend many years later. 'She had an air of reserve which we mistook for hauteur. Afterwards we realized that it was only shyness, and beneath it she was the most human person in the world.' Human certainly, but Princess Marina's fundamental shyness, which even as an adult she never entirely lost, was often misinterpreted for hauteur. But since she was also capable of pulling rank and becoming immensely grand, particularly with those she considered her inferior, it was an easy mistake to make. Among the girls at Princess Mestchersky's Finishing School, however, Marina was invariably considered 'the tops'. It was said that 'she would fly into battle in defence of some girl who was out of favour with the rest, not caring whether she made herself disliked or not. They were rather in awe of her sharp wit. Her knowledge of the world and of human nature made her seem different from themselves ....'

As a boarder, Princess Marina's day began with prayers at 8am, followed by breakfast half an hour later. At 9 she and the rest of the girls were allowed to walk in the Bois de Boulogne for an hour, after which morning studies began. French language, history and literature, for example, might be followed by talks on subjects as diverse as China and Chinese art or the industrial development of Great Britain. Lunch was taken at 1pm sharp and until teatime, three and a half hours later, afternoons would be spent visiting places of interest such as the Louvre, or the palaces of Versailles or Fontainebleau. Lectures followed by 'prep' occupied the late afternoon, and dinner was always served on the stroke of 7.30pm. After that, evenings would often be taken up with visits to the theatre or to concerts, not simply for entertainment, but to help broaden the girls' appreciation of the performing arts.

In early 1924, during her first term at Princess Mestchersky's, Marina learned there was soon to be a new addition to the family and that she was about to become an aunt. News that Olga was expecting her first baby that August was rapturously received in Paris, and in May, when Prince and Princess Paul, as they were formally known, spent two weeks at the Nicholas's apartment while *en route* to England, the family's obvious joy was sufficient cause for further celebration.

Determined that he and Olga should spend the summer in England, where he was anxious for the baby to be born, Prince Paul rented Bisham

Grange, a picturesque cottage near Marlow in Buckinghamshire, for the first six weeks of their stay. Then, in June, during Royal Ascot, the highlight of the British racing calendar and the sporting high point of the royal family's year, the Duchess of York suggested that Paul and Olga might like to stay at White Lodge in Richmond Park during August and September for Olga's confinement. White Lodge – where Queen Mary had been born to the Duke and Duchess of Teck and where she, in turn, gave birth to her first child, the future King Edward VIII – had been given to the Duke and Duchess of York when they were married in April 1923. Prince Paul, overwhelmed by their friend Elizabeth York's offer, immediately accepted.

On 7 August the expectant parents drove to Richmond and there, on the thirteenth, Olga gave birth to a son. One month later their absent hosts, the York's, interrupted their annual summer holiday at Balmoral to attend the christening of the infant Prince Alexander. The ceremony at White Lodge, like Paul and Olga's wedding in Belgrade not quite a year before, was performed according to the rites of the Greek Orthodox Church. Princess Marina, together with her parents and sister Elizabeth, who were again in London for the 'Season', were naturally among the guests; so, too, were King Alexander of Serbia and the Infanta Beatrice of Spain who, along with the Duke of York, stood as godparents to the four-week-old prince.

That summer Marina, now technically a dèbutante in her own right, took a far more active part in the round of social events in London than had been the case a year earlier and she also accompanied her parents when they were the guests of the Marquess and Marchioness Curzon at Hackwood Park at Basingstoke, the Duke and Duchess of Portland at Welbeck Abbey in Nottinghamshire, and Lord Ivor Churchill at Blenheim Palace, the Oxfordshire seat of the dukes of Marlborough. Then, the 'ball' was suddenly over and it was time for the princess to return to Paris. Marina went back to school to finish her education, while Princess Nicholas resumed her involvement with the relief agencies she had established to ease the plight of Russian émigrés, thousands of whom had settled in Paris after fleeing the Revolution. Of all the organizations she had helped establish or was otherwise connected with in some way, however, Princess Nicholas was especially attached to two residential homes in particular. One of them set up by Dorothy Paget, the wealthy daughter of Almeric Paget, 1st Baron Queensborough and his American wife, Pauline Whitney, was at the Château de la Cossonnerie at Saint Geneviève-des-Bois, where she also financed the establishment of the Russian Orthodox Cemetery. In time, many notable Russians would be buried there, among them Princess Nicholas's own brother Grand Duke Andrei Vladimirovich and his wife the ballerina and former mistress of the young Nicholas II, Mathilde Kschessinkaya, Princess Vera Mestchersky, the founder of Marina's finishing school, which Dorothy Paget had also attended, Prince Felix Yusupov, one of Rasputin's assassins and his wife Irina, and, though very much later on, the legendary ballet dancer, director and choreographer, Rudolf Nureyev.

Like her mother, Princess Marina was a frequent visitor to the elderly residents at the Château de la Cossonnerie or 'la Maison Russe' (the 'Russian House') as it was also known. Indeed, during the early 1950s the writer Jennifer Ellis recalled having watched her on one occasion '... helping an old lady who was trying to knit a pair of gloves and had got into difficulties. The Princess's sleek brown head was bent close to the white one; her face was set in concentration. But she was still young enough to be unable to hide the flicker of amusement in her eyes as she unravelled a thumb at least four times too big for any human hand.'

The other home which most concerned Princess Nicholas was the one she herself had founded. If Dorothy Paget had taken pity on men and women who had once known only privilege, Princess Nicholas's compassion drew no such distinction. Deeply concerned by the fact that refugee children were left to fend for themselves while their parents took whatever work they could find, and disturbed by images of orphans begging in the streets, Princess Nicholas, who sold some of her jewellery to help fund her charity work, acquired a large property at St Germain-en-Laye in the western suburbs of Paris. Under her supervision the house was soon functioning as a home and kindergarten, caring for sixty children ranging in age from two to twelve years old. Of the new inhabitants, some were able to claim noble descent while others were the children of men and women who had once been servants in imperial or aristocratic households. At Princess Nicholas's insistence, neither background nor class was to have any place at the home for, as she wisely pointed out, 'When they grow up they will have to work, so what is the use of starting them off with false ideas? And besides, children should never be made conscious of social differences.'

Twice a year the princess would organize a ball, a fête or a bazaar to raise funds for her 'Home for Russian Children' and in arranging the events she would enlist the help of her daughters and their friends. Even the family's chauffeur and their four servants were roped in to lend a hand, while at the Nicholases' apartment on the Boulevard Jules Sandeau one room was turned into an office where Princess Nicholas, Marina and Elizabeth would spend long hours hard at work. Though she was always a willing member of her mother's team, Marina nevertheless made no secret of the fact that she much preferred being of practical assistance at the children's home itself. Strongly maternal, she was in her element when playing games with the older children, and at bath time, when it came to getting the 'babies', as the two-, three- and four-year-olds were called, ready for bed.

Paris was a city for which Princess Marina always held a deep affection – and not without good reason for, had the Greek monarchy been more stable, the vitally important years of her youth and early adulthood would have been stifled by restrictive codes of royal protocol and diplomatic convention. As it was, exile, despite its disadvantages, afforded Marina the freedom and anonymity in which to grow and develop as an individual unrestricted by the cloistered atmosphere of court life.

CHAPTER SIX
TOTO AND PRINCE GEORGE

Soon after she had completed her year at Princess Mestchersky's school in 1925, Princess Marina travelled to Rome to visit her uncle Prince Christopher. After the death of his wife two years earlier, the prince had been on a mission to find a house in the city suitable for himself and his mother, the dowager Queen Olga. He found what he was looking for in a villa that was owned by the Irish-born Baroness Aliotti. From the house, or the Villa Anastasia as the prince re-named it in tribute to his late wife, with its 'sunny loggias, terraces and big garden', commanding a panoramic view of Rome, Marina as well as her elder sister Elizabeth or 'Woolly' as she was nicknamed in childhood, were introduced by 'Uncle Christo' to the cream of Italian society. This Roman interlude marked the start of yet another round of travels for Princess Marina, one that was briefly interrupted by the death on 18 June 1926 of her seventy-five-year old grandmother, Queen Olga.

In his memoirs first published in 1938, Prince Christopher recalled several psychic experiences he had had in his life. One of them concerned the final days of his mother's life. The Villa Anastasia, he wrote, 'was built in the form of an L', which meant that he could see Queen Olga's rooms from his own. 'I had returned from a party late one night', he recalled, 'and on throwing back my shutters before getting into bed, I saw both her windows brilliantly illuminated. It was 2am, and I wondered vaguely why she should be awake at that hour, and then I noticed that the light was not like that from a night-light or an ordinary electric lamp. It was a golden glow that seemed to fill the whole room.

'Next morning I asked her what she had been doing awake at that time of night, but she answered in surprise that she had never slept better in her life, and had not once turned on the light. I saw the strange light once more, and then left for Florence to stay with Queen Sophie, and forgot all about it. But one morning I awoke with an extraordinary premonition that I ought to leave for Rome .... I started immediately and arrived ... to find my mother placidly having tea on the terrace with my sister .... But the next day my mother was taken ill, and in less than a week she had gone to join my father.

'The night she died the golden glow was there again, a glorious golden light, full of promise of the reward to come.'

Following her funeral service in Rome, Queen Olga's coffin was placed alongside that of her eldest son Constantine, in the crypt of the Russian church in Florence, where the red damask walls were hung with gold and silver icons, and the blue and white Greek flag was draped across the ceiling. When, in due course, the Greek monarchy was restored yet again, Queen Olga, King Constantine and, by then, Queen Sophie, who died in January 1932, were accorded a triple state funeral in Athens, after which they were interred in the private royal burial ground at Tatoi.

In the spring of 1927, Paul and Olga again decided to spend the summer in England; and for the duration of their visit rented Viscount Ednam's house on Cheyne Walk in Chelsea. Princess Marina was invited to accompany her sister and brother-in-law, and at one point it almost looked as though she was about to win the heart of the Prince of Wales who, according to Neil Balfour in his biography of his father-in-law, Prince Paul, 'appeared to take an unusual interest in her.' The prince's attentions were apparently 'more than passing and went far beyond the call of duty and politeness. Paul was near certain and Marina completely overwhelmed, whilst Olga and her mother scarcely dared hope.'

At almost twenty-one, Princess Marina was now even more striking to look at. In addition, she had not only developed the Parisienne's flair for fashion, but also a polished sophistication, that would certainly work to her advantage if considered as a possible Princess of Wales. The Greek word *porphyrogenitos* – 'born under the purple' – summarized the dignity and style of Marina's bearing. Despite all the excitement and raised hopes, however, the Prince of Wales lost interest and retreated to the arms of his long-standing mistress Freda Dudley-Ward, the wife of Liberal Member of Parliament, William Dudley Ward. How Princess Marina reacted to the heir apparent's strange behaviour is not clear. But if Princess Nicholas was crestfallen that her youngest daughter no longer stood the remotest chance with the future king of England, she was to be equally miffed when her middle daughter Elizabeth failed to arouse so much as a flicker of interest in the future king of Italy.

Though Princess Nicholas, for all her pride in her impressive imperial Romanov ancestry cannot be said to have made an especially prestigious marriage herself, she was never less than ambitious for her daughters. She would, in fact, have preferred all three to have married kings. With her abortive engagement to Crown Prince Frederick, five years before, Olga had at least stood a fleeting chance of one day becoming queen of Denmark. Marina, had things progressed further, might conceivably have bagged the Prince of Wales and, but for the fact that Elizabeth had been paraded too obviously in front of Crown Prince Umberto, it is not unreasonable to suppose that Princess Nicholas may just have secured a consort's crown for at least one of her offspring.

In the meantime, while Princess Elizabeth and her match-making mother were staying with the Italian royal family at the Villa D'Este during the summer of 1928, Marina, Paul, and a heavily pregnant Olga were once more in London. Arriving shortly before Olga's second confinement, Prince Paul, feeling like 'an old dowager chaperoning her grandchildren', escorted Marina to many of the social events that for the fourth consecutive 'Season' filled up her diary. *The* event for which both Prince and Princess Paul had waited so eagerly occurred on 29 June, when Olga gave birth to her second son. At his christening a few weeks later, he was named Nicholas in honour of his grandfather.

With two grandchildren and a son-in-law whose praises he could not sing loudly enough, the elder Prince Nicholas soon began teasing Marina and Elizabeth about their own marital prospects. Despite the family's subtle – and not so subtle – attempts to find them suitable husbands, they were both still single. Did they want to become old maids, Prince Nicholas asked? Neither princess rose to the bait. Instead, they simply assured their father, 'We don't want to get married yet.' Within five years both had changed their minds.

Not long after their own marriage, Prince and Princess Paul had been offered their very first home together, far away from the dull royal palace they shared with the king and queen of Yugoslavia in Belgrade. Known as the Ermitage, the three-storey, timber chalet, which had been a royal shooting lodge, was to be found at the top of the picturesque village of Bohinj Jezero, high in the Julian Alps. In what soon became something of a tradition, Olga's family spent part of every summer at Bohinj for many years, enjoying the beauty of the surrounding countryside and relaxing after their activities in the capital cities of Europe. In September 1933 there was scarcely any alteration to the established order at the Ermitage, save for the presence of a rather reserved thirty-three-year-old, with whom Paul and Olga, Marina and Elizabeth, had spent most of their time during a visit to Munich earlier that year.

'Toto' Toerring, or more correctly, His Illustrious Highness Carl Theodor Klemens, Count zu Toerring-Jettenbach, a member of the Wittelsbach family, and a nephew of Queen Elisabeth of the Belgians, had been earmarked by Prince and Princess Paul as a possible husband for 'Woolly'. While they seemed to be quietly attracted to one another, Toto had given no definite indication of his feelings towards the least well known of Prince Nicholas's daughters and it was felt a gentle nudge might help things along; hence his invitation to Bohinj. Shortly after his arrival, Paul, Olga and Marina conveniently slipped away to London, leaving Toto and Woolly in the company of her parents and Uncle Christo, but otherwise quite alone. The ruse worked and on 22 September Toto proposed and Elizabeth accepted. They were married four months later, on 10 January 1934, in the chapel of Seefeld Castle, near Munich.

Of that close circle of girl cousins who had shared the game of 'Keeping House' on a Greek island many years before, only Marina, who was now twenty-seven, and the late King Constantine's daughters Irene, who was twenty-nine and Katherine, who was now twenty, were unmarried. Olga and Elizabeth had found Paul and Toto; Princess Helen, though they were now divorced, had married Carol of Romania; while Margarita, Theodora, Cecile and Sophie, the four daughters of Marina's uncle Prince

Andrew, had taken as their respective husbands, Gottfried, 8th Prince of Hohenlohe-Langenburg; Berthold, Margrave of Baden; Georg Donatus, Hereditary Grand Duke of Hesse and by Rhine, and Prince Christoph of Hesse.

In his study of Princess Marina published in 1962, James Wentworth-Day wrote that, after the wedding of Woolly and Toto, an unidentified friend made the following floridly sentimental observation of the bride's younger sister: 'The starry look in [Elizabeth's] eyes stirred something deep and, so far, unknown in Marina. From a lively, carefree girl she seemed to have grown into wistful womanhood. Her face acquired a new spiritual expression. She read more, she thought, perhaps she dreamt. This period of sudden spiritual growth was a vital one in her young life, and she herself must have been aware of it.

'I suddenly understood the change which had struck me in Princess Marina. I understood that the girl with those golden-brown eyes was a dreamer and a thinker. She was also an idealist; and she was hoping for these ideals and dreams to come true. I feel that she was capable of great feeling, and that the decisive moment had come for her.'

Talk of Marina as a 'girl' and one who was 'a dreamer and a thinker' seems at odds with the alternative image of a reasonably worldly woman of almost thirty. Perhaps there had been some kind of noticeable change in Marina at that time, 'spiritual' or otherwise. But it could also be argued without recourse to purple prose that a single woman, especially the youngest in a closely united family, might very well experience deep emotion, even introspection, when the last of her siblings marries and she is left on her own.

Whatever Princess Marina may or may not have discovered about herself following the marriage of Elizabeth and Toto, her own 'decisive moment' was soon to manifest itself in the physical shape of Prince George, the fourth and youngest surviving son of King George V and Queen Mary. As with her parents, Marina was no stranger to the British royal family. But how well she herself actually knew them is open to question. 'I am sure we shall like Marina & that she will be a charming addition to the family', is how Queen Mary wrote to George V, when she and their youngest son became engaged. Yet even allowing for the fact that the queen found it very difficult to communicate with other women, even within her own family, this rather distant reference to the princess who was also her goddaughter, does suggest that Marina wasn't on an intimate footing with any of them. Other early encounters with her distant royal cousins seemed to have been equally vague. The interest which the Prince of Wales had shown in Marina during her visit to London in 1927, for example, appeared to have developed remarkably suddenly, almost as if they had never met before. Nor is it certain that Prince George had ever been particularly aware of his future wife until the late summer of 1933.

That September, while Count Toerring was making up his mind about 'Woolly' at Bohinj, Marina accompanied Prince and Princess Paul to London. The main reason for their visit was to take their elder son Alexander back to school, though Paul never needed an excuse to find himself in England looking up old friends. Society hostess Emerald Cunard, like the Duke and Duchess of York, and indeed Prince George himself, was just one such friend. Princess Marina met Prince George at a lunch party that month given by Lady Cunard. They established an instant rapport which led to several more meetings. Even so, by the time Marina left London with Olga and Paul at the end of that particular visit, there were no signs of a blossoming romance. On the contrary, Prince George, who had quite a forceful personality himself, declared that he found Marina too 'bossy'.

It is always possible that this very bossiness was one of the traits George decided he liked in Marina. For when she returned the following spring to stay with her sister and brother-in-law at Claridge's, Prince George was among the first to call. On the first of his many visits, however, bad timing meant that he had to while away several hours with Prince Paul – whom he had ostensibly dropped in to see – while Marina and Olga were out shopping. At length Princess Paul returned to the hotel, but without her sister. Marina, she explained, had gone on to the hairdressers. As the hours ticked by, it became abundantly clear that George had no other engagements that day, and was in no great hurry to leave. When at long last Marina did appear, Prince George's delight was all too obvious, not only to the princess herself but also to Olga and Paul.

For the rest of her stay Marina and George lunched and dined together; went to the theatre and cinema; danced at the Embassy Club in Bond Street; walked unnoticed in Green Park; visited the Prince of Wales at Fort Belvedere, his crenallated private retreat on the edge of Windsor Great Park at Virginia Water in Sunningdale; and went for long, fast drives in George's sports car. As the dynamics changed between them, George, by now totally enchanted, said of Marina, 'She is the one woman with whom I could be happy to spend the rest of my life. We laugh at the same sort of thing. She beats me at most games and doesn't give a damn how fast I drive when I take her out in the car.'

When Marina left London shortly afterwards to join her mother at a health spa at Savoie in the French Alps, she wasn't certain when she would next see 'Georgie'. But as with Woolly and Toto, though Marina was not aware of it, Prince Paul had already invited George to visit Bohinj that summer. And, of course, Marina would be there.

Like Royal Ascot, Cowes week on the Solent off the Isle of Wight, was always a popular sporting fixture in the British royal family's calendar. But since Cowes, which remains one of the world's longest-running annual regattas, meant boats rather than horses, *the* royal passion, past and present, of course, fewer members of the royal family attended. In early August 1934, however, Prince George who enjoyed the sailing as much as the onshore social events that went with it was one royal visitor. It was from there that he cabled Prince Paul to say that he planned to arrive in Bohinj on the sixteenth of the month and almost as soon as Cowes week had ended, George borrowed an aircraft from his eldest brother the Prince of Wales, who had become the very first of Britain's royal pilots, and flew off in the direction of the Yugoslav airfield at Ljubljana, *en route* to Bohinj.

Arriving at the 'Ermitage' a day ahead of him was Marina's uncle Prince Christopher. As soon as Paul, Olga and Marina heard that George was about to join them, 'Christo' received 'a mysterious SOS', telling him to 'get into the next train and come to Bohinj'. Fearing some sort of catastrophe, the prince immediately telephoned. Princess Olga answered and, in great excitement, explained the situation. 'Do you remember you were with us when Elizabeth got engaged to Toto?' she asked. 'They are both so happy that I have an idea you will bring Marina luck too.'

Though often quoted from his memoirs over the years, no biography of Princess Marina would be complete without the inclusion of at least part of Prince Christopher's description of what happened at Bohinj.

'The weather was glorious', he wrote, 'and we spent the next few days in shooting, fishing, rambling through the woods and motoring over to luncheon or tea with my brother Nicholas and his wife, who had taken a villa twenty-five miles away. The atmosphere grew more and more electric. Then one evening we all played backgammon in the sitting-room until we could hardly keep awake. One by one we departed for bed until George and Marina were left sitting alone at opposite ends of the sofa.

'I had been in my bedroom for about half an hour when I discovered that I had left my cigarette-case on the backgammon table. Putting on my dressing-gown I went in search of it. The door of the sitting-room was open; George and Marina were still seated on the sofa, though no longer ... at the opposite ends of it. I stole back to bed without my case.'

Next day the prince and princess announced their engagement to Marina's family; though until King George V responded to his son's message seeking formal consent to the marriage, as members of the royal family were required to do in accordance with the Royal Marriages Act of 1772, the couple's news had to remain a secret.

In Scotland where they were on their summer holiday at Balmoral, George V and Queen Mary were delighted by George's news and, on the evening of 28 August, an archaically-worded formal statement was released to the news media to the effect that it was 'with the greatest pleasure' that the King and Queen announced 'the betrothal of their dearly beloved son the Prince George to the Princess Marina, daughter of the Prince and Princess Nicholas of Greece, to which union the King has gladly given his consent.'

CHAPTER SEVEN
A KING'S SON

Prince George of Wales, as he was first known, was born at Sandringham on 20 December 1902. Thus, unlike his three elder brothers who were born during the reign of their great-grandmama Queen Victoria, Prince George was an Edwardian. His grandfather, King Edward VII, was about to enter the third year of his reign at the time of George's birth.

On reflection, the idea of Prince George as an Edwardian somehow seems very appropriate. For the era that took his grandfather's name was a more romantic era associated with colour and innovation, freedom of expression and freedom of style, overlaid with a certain naughty frivolity, a world removed from the sombre mood that epitomized all but the first twenty years of Victoria's reign. A man of his time, George was well suited to romance, colour, style and frivolity, even though some of the 'naughtier' aspects of his adult life would give rise to serious concern.

York Cottage, in the grounds of Sandringham House, near King's Lynn in Norfolk, where Prince George was born, was originally known as the Bachelor's Cottage and still stands on the edge of the 'Lower Pond', one of the royal estate's two artificial lakes. Built by Edward VII when he was Prince of Wales, as guest accommodation, this relatively small, two-storey house had subsequently been given to Prince George's father, then Duke of York, as a wedding present, and was renamed in his honour.

Stuffed full of heavy 'modern' furniture from the fashionable London firm of Maple's, overheated in winter, suffocating in summer, and permeated by cooking smells whatever the season, York Cottage was for thirty-three years the favourite residence of the Duke and Duchess of York, even after they became King George V and Queen Mary. Ill-proportioned for the growing family that lived there, the house was made up of a small entrance hall, the duke's study or 'library', two medium-sized drawing rooms, a dining room, and a billiard room. Upstairs the duke and duchess each had a bedroom and dressing room; two or three further rooms were set aside for the use of equerries and ladies in waiting while, tucked away behind a swing door, were the day and night nurseries. All the York children slept in the night nursery, as did their nanny, 'Lala' Bill.

Prince George's father, another Prince George, was the second son of 'Bertie' and 'Alix', Prince and Princess of Wales, who on the death of Queen Victoria in January 1901, became King Edward VII and Queen Alexandra. In July 1893, when he was twenty-eight, Bertie and Alix's son George, who had been created Duke of York just over a year before, married the twenty-six-year-old Princess Victoria Mary of Teck, or 'May' as she was known. The only daughter of Queen Victoria's cousin, the enormously-popular Princess Mary Adelaide of Cambridge, known to the Victorian public as 'Fat Mary', and her husband, Prince Francis (Franz), Duke of Teck, Princess May had first been engaged to George's elder brother, Albert Victor, Duke of Clarence and Avondale and earl of Athlone, known within the family as 'Eddy'. Slow, indolent and unmotivated, his gentleness had irritated his father as much as it had endeared him to his over indulgent mother, known to her children as 'Motherdear'.

'Among the few things Prince Eddy really cared for,' James Pope-Hennessy would write in his official biography of Queen Mary, 'was every form of dissipation and amusement'. The stories and rumours were legion, from Eddy frequenting a male brothel in Cleveland Street in the West End to unfounded claims that he was Victorian London's notorious serial killer, Jack the Ripper. As was often the case in those days, the assumed steadying influence of marriage was regarded as the cure-all for young men of Eddy's disposition and May of Teck, though excessively shy and reserved, was seen as the perfect candidate for the role of Eddy's wife and in the fullness of time, his queen. Though not a love match, Eddy proposed, May accepted and the wedding was arranged to take place on 27 February 1892. Then, only six weeks before the event fate diverted the course of history. At Sandringham on 6 January, Eddy fell victim to the flu pandemic that recurred throughout 1889-92. Within three days, influenza had developed into pneumonia and on 14 January, six days after his twenty-eighth birthday, he died.

For Princess May, however, the future remained unchanged. Approved by Queen Victoria as a suitable queen consort for Eddy, his brother George was now encouraged to think in terms of marrying May. Over the next sixteen months, drawn together first by shared mourning, 'Georgie' and May's affection for one another steadily grew to the point at which, on 3 May 1893, while visiting the duke's sister Princess Louise, Duchess of Fife, for tea at her house near Richmond, it was suggested that George should take May into the garden 'to look at the frogs in the pond.'

'We walked together ... in the garden,' May noted in her diary that evening, 'and he proposed to me, & I accepted him. Louise and MacDuff [the Duke of Fife] were delighted. I drove home to announce the news to Mama and Papa & Georgie followed .... We telegraphed to all the relations.'

Two months later, on 6 July, Prince George, Duke of York and Princess May of Teck were married in the Chapel Royal at St James's Palace. To Queen Victoria who sat, draped in lace and fanning herself, near the altar on that sultry afternoon, the Chapel Royal, even though it was where she and her 'Dearest Albert' had been married in February 1840, was 'small & *very* ugly'. St George's Chapel, Windsor, she declared, 'is lovely for a marriage in summer.'

That afternoon in what was an extraordinary lapse of taste and sensitivity, given that Eddy had died there so recently, the Duke of York took his new wife off to Sandringham and a honeymoon at York Cottage. Even Queen Victoria commented that the choice of venue seemed 'rather *unlucky* and sad.' But as we have already seen George's love affair with York Cottage started at this time and would be his and May's much loved home for over thirty years. It was also there that five of their six children were born. Like Queen Victoria, the Duchess of York found everything to do with pregnancy, childbirth and babies distasteful, not least because of all the unwelcome attention she received. Among the members of the royal family who were astonished by May's unwillingness to indulge in baby talk was Queen Victoria's eldest daughter Vicky, the future Empress Frederick of Germany, who couldn't have been more interested in every detail 'connected with the birth of so celestial a being as a human baby'.

After visiting May, whom she declared to be 'unmaternal', Vicky told her mother that 'She ... does not wish it remarked or mentioned.'

Nevertheless, by the end of the century, May had already given her husband three children: Edward, or 'David', as he was known, who was born just before his parents' first wedding anniversary; Albert, otherwise 'Bertie', who would one day reign as King George VI; and Victoria, the future Princess Royal, who was always known as Mary, the last of her four names. Henry or 'Harry', the Yorks' third son was born when the 20th-century century was but three months old, and Prince George, the future Duke of Kent, one of our two players, followed on 20 December 1902, just four years almost to the day, before his future wife Princess Marina. The youngest of the Yorks' children was Prince John. Born not quite three years after Prince George, he was not only mentally slower than his siblings, but was also epileptic. As a result, and as was so often the case in those days, the young prince lived apart from the rest of his family. Out of sight, though not out of mind, 'Johnnie' lived at Wood Farm on the Sandringham estate where until his death at the age of not quite fourteen, he was cared for by the family's devoted nanny, 'Lala' Bill.

In later years, whenever the four surviving princes and their sister recalled their childhood, Sandringham always stood out in sharp focus, as indeed did their indulgent grandparents, King Edward VII and Queen Alexandra, who lived up at the 'Big House', a quarter of a mile away through the park.

Before David and Bertie were sent off to the Royal Naval Colleges at Osborne and Dartmouth, they, like Princess Mary, were educated privately at York Cottage. Like them, George and Harry's education also began there. Later on, while Harry was sent to Eton, his younger brother went off to St Peter's Court Preparatory School at Broadstairs, on the south coast. At the time of Prince George's engagement to Princess Marina, the Marquess of Donegall, a fellow pupil at St Peter's, recalled one particularly human impression of the schoolboy prince. In the *Sunday Dispatch* of 2 September 1934 he wrote, 'In those days Prince George, in contrast to his well-groomed appearance in later years, had an obstinate tuft of hair on the top of his head which refused to obey brush or comb. When more than usually puzzled over how long it would take A, B and C to do the traditional 'piece of work', he would curl the recalcitrant tuft with the index finger of his left hand. This appeared to produce the required inspiration.'

Of the surviving four royal brothers, Prince George was academically the brightest. In fact, school reports from A.J. Richardson, his headmaster, were so pleasing that the prince's parents went to St Peter's in person to thank him. 'But, sir' said Richardson to the boy's father, 'Prince George applies himself to every subject. It is a joy to teach such a child.' Unfortunately, the same could not be said of either David or Bertie who were repeatedly admonished for their lack of application and poor exam results; while Harry, afterwards Duke of Gloucester, was an even poorer student. 'Do for goodness sake wake up and work harder and use the brains God has given you,' wrote his exasperated mother when he was still at Eton. 'All you write about is your everlasting football of which I am heartily sick.'

In November 1901, ten months after the death of Queen Victoria and the accession of Edward VII, George, Duke of York was created Prince of Wales, the title traditionally held by the heir apparent. But unlike his father, on whom the style and rank was bestowed one month after his birth in 1841, and which he held for almost sixty years, Prince George, as Prince of Wales, was to be King-in-waiting for less than a decade. On 6 May 1910 Edward VII died, six months short of his sixty-ninth birthday.

The coronation of the new King George V and Queen Mary (as Georgie and May had now become) took place at Westminster Abbey on 22 June the following year. Witnessing the epic ritual from the front row of the royal gallery near the high altar, were four of their children, Bertie, Mary, Harry and George. David, who had succeeded his father as the twentieth Prince of Wales, played his own part in the ceremony when, as heir to the throne, he knelt before the King to swear allegiance. If, however, the princes had behaved impeccably in the abbey, the same was not true afterwards when all hell broke loose during the return procession to Buckingham Palace. The diarist Lord Crawford wrote, 'One of the great successes of the Coronation was a stand-up fight between the two kilted princes [George and Harry, then aged nine and eleven respectively].... By some imprudence the Prince of Wales and his sister were sent in a state coach with the younger brothers but without a controlling prelate or pedagogue. When fairly started from the Abbey, a free fight began to the huge delight of the spectators in Whitehall. The efforts of Princess Mary to mollify the combatants were sincere but ineffectual, and during the strife she nearly had her sweet little coronet knocked off! Peace was ultimately restored after about fifty yards of hullaballoo.'

Another significant royal event that summer, was David's ceremonial investiture at Caernarvon Castle as Prince of Wales. It was the nearest he would ever come to being crowned. At this time, the prince was in his second year at Dartmouth as a naval cadet and though the meaning of his investiture and the reasons for it being a public spectacle were clear to him, other theatrical aspects of the ceremony caused embarrassment. Chief among them was the satin and velvet ermine-trimmed costume he was obliged to wear. Throughout his career as heir apparent – the 'Golden Boy of Empire' as he would become popularly known – and during his brief eleven month reign as King Edward VIII, David was among the most democratically inclined princes. Because of this, as he claimed in a television interview forty years after his abdication, his seismic clash with the British Establishment had been 'inevitable'.

Though Prince George was never to offer a direct challenge to the established view of monarchy, he was every bit as democratic as his eldest brother, and just as much an individual. There were naturally marked differences in their characters, but even so they were very alike in other respects. They shared the same sense of humour, the same energy and the same passion for keeping fit. They had very similar tastes in music, especially jazz which George would belt out on the piano at his brother's country house, Fort Belvedere on the edge of Windsor Great Park at weekend parties, they were both mimics and impersonators, they adored night life, and though not to their credit, had a penchant for forming undesirable relationships. Yet, in his brother David also found a kind of mentor; one to whom he could unburden himself in complete trust and confidence. In his memoirs *A King's Story*, the by-now Duke of Windsor wrote, 'Although George was eight and a half years my junior, I found in his character qualities that were akin to my own ... we became more than brothers – we became close friends'.

Not long before his fourteenth birthday in 1916, Prince George embarked on what was arguably the unhappiest period of his life. Right from the start he was horrified at the thought of having to follow David and Bertie into the Royal Navy. Indeed, the biographer James Wentworth-Day had even claimed that the prince's fondness for wearing a kilt had led him to hope that he might be permitted to join a Highland regiment. True or not, George's immediate future had been settled for him by the Lord High Admiral in person; in other words, by his father. In an attempt to dissuade her husband from sending Georgie to naval college, Queen Mary tried to make the King understand that it might do the boy more harm than good. It was unusual for the queen to intercede on her children's behalf at any time since, as she said herself, she had to always to remember that their father was also their king – and they were all his subjects. In this instance, however, Queen Mary made an exception. Of all her children, she saw much of herself reflected in Prince George, not least in their shared appreciation of the Arts. How well the queen came to know and understand her sons and daughter is a moot point, but she was the first to realize the error of sending this particular son into an environment that his sensitive and artistic temperament would find completely alien. In the event, Queen Mary's argument fell on deaf ears. The king would not be moved. An aesthete Prince George might be, but a sailor he would become. On that note, the prince was packed off to the junior naval college at Osborne on the Isle of Wight.

At least to begin with, he seemed to settle in, applying himself dutifully to his studies and achieving far higher grades than either David or Bertie before him. But then, through boredom or unhappiness, perhaps both, Prince George's concentration waned and, from the top of the scholastic ladder, he began slipping towards the bottom –where, incidentally, his brothers were always to be found. Languages were to prove George's saving grace, however. Four years after leaving the senior naval academy at Dartmouth in Devon, he attended a course at the Royal Naval College at Greenwich, in south east London. There he gained first place in French and second in Italian in the voluntary examination in foreign languages for Acting Sub-Lieutenants. Later still, his proficiency was further acknowledged, when his duties started to include those of interpreter in French.

Yet whatever services Prince George was able to offer the Navy, the Navy was to disrupt his health. Sea-sickness and insomnia plagued him from the start of his first voyage and, in 1929, were greatly to contribute to his being relieved of the career his father had so ruthlessly imposed on him. In the years between George had no choice but to make the most of a very disagreeable situation. In April 1920, at the age of seventeen, he passed out of Dartmouth, and nine months later, newly promoted to the rank of midshipman, he was detailed to HMS *Iron Duke*, flagship of the Mediterranean fleet. Service aboard HMS *Queen Elizabeth* and the flotilla leader HMS *Mackay* then followed and, with subsequent promotion, he was appointed in turn to HMS *Hawkins*, the flagship in China; HMS *Nelson*, flagship of the Home Fleet, and HMS *Durban*.

Though Prince George's service career caused him many regrets, life was not without its compensations. Nor, indeed, did 'PG' or 'Babe' as he was known, ever lose his sense of humour. In *Princess Marina: Her Life and Times* Stella King wrote, 'Once in China, some press cameramen, hearing that British royalty was about, met him when he was about to board his ship and asked if he had seen the 'King of England'. Without hesitation he gestured behind him towards the ship's doctor, a heavily-built man who was being carried in a sedan chair, and left them to sort it out for themselves. He laughed a great deal when the portly doctor's picture appeared in a newspaper later with a caption saying that he was the "English King".'

Despite amusing episodes like this, the undisputed rewards of visiting far-flung places and the camaraderie of the ship's company, Prince George continued to petition his father for permission to leave the Royal Navy. Though the king would have none of it, George refused to let go of the hope that he might be allowed to do something more constructive with his life and by 1928 that ambition was closer to being fulfilled than he realized. During Royal Ascot week that year Mabell, Countess of Airlie, who had frequently acted as confessor to the children of her old friend Queen Mary, was staying at Windsor Castle in her capacity as lady-in-waiting; a post she had held ever since 'May' became Princess of Wales. At dinner one evening, the dowager countess was seated next to Prince George, who told her how much he was dreading his next voyage. Some thirty years later, when she published her autobiography, *Thatched with Gold,* Lady Airlie recalled, 'He was not happy in the Navy and wanted to go into the Civil Service or the Foreign Office, but the King would not hear of it. His only reason for refusing is that it has never been done before,' the Prince said. 'I've tried to make him see that I'm not cut out for the Navy, but it's no use. What can I do?' I advised him not to waste time in arguing with the King – which would only make him angry – but to work hard while he was at sea, get the Civil Service papers and do them, and then let his father see the results. He told me some time later that he had acted on my advice, and that it had been successful.'

George V's change of heart was not due so much to the results of his son's civil service exams, but more persuasively to medical reports that made it clear that Prince George's digestive trouble would severely undermine his health, were he to be forced to continue in the navy. A year later the prince was promoted to the rank of commander and, to his profound relief, finally discharged from the service.

For the next three years, the king's son – the first prince ever to have become a civil servant – was attached to the Foreign Office. His duties there, however, did not prove sufficiently demanding. Like the Prince of Wales, George had a tremendous liking and admiration for the working man. And like David, he not only became interested in social and industrial conditions, but shared his brother's deep concern for the misery of the unemployed who, by 1931, totalled more than two million. It was this very real social conscience, formed largely through his experiences in the navy, which led Prince George to change departments within the civil service. From his desk at the Foreign Office, overlooking St James's Park, he moved along Whitehall to the Home Office. This move, arranged by Sir Herbert Samuel, the home secretary, and Sir Malcolm Delevigne, permanent under-secretary of state, resulted in George becoming a Home Office Factory Inspector. In his initial report to Sir Herbert, Delevigne itemized the scope of the prince's duties, notwithstanding the king's instruction that his son should remain available for royal engagements as and when required. He wrote, 'As his work will lie in the Metropolitan area we would propose to attach him to three London districts, Southwark, Woolwich and South Essex, in order to give him as interesting a range of work as possible and at the same time allow of some concentration of interest in the more important and live issues of factory administration .... Among the more important and live issues to which his attention might be given are the work of the London docks (loading and unloading of ships, which are processes fruitful of accident and are governed by an elaborate code of regulations, and which happen to be, at the moment, the subject of international discussion); the asbestos industry with its newly discovered dangers to health; different branches of the engineering and woodworking industries; the building industry with its recently amended code of safety regulations, etc. It would also be arranged to let him see interesting developments in health and welfare work.... the actual visiting of the factories should be alternated with visits to the Home Office Industrial Museum ... where he would be given some intensive instruction in the principles and practice of the safeguarding of machinery and the prevention of various kinds of accidents; the nature and prevention of industrial diseases and the promotion of industrial health and welfare; the principles of factory ventilation and lights; and so on. This is now part of the ordinary training of recruits to the Factory Inspectorate.'

With the full approval of both the king and the prime minister, Stanley Baldwin, Prince George joined the Home Office on 12 April 1932. From the start George took to his new occupation as if born to it. In many respects, the prince's work complemented that of another of his brothers. Motivated by a very same wish to be of practical benefit to the ordinary man, 'Bertie', otherwise Prince Albert, Duke of York, had already become involved with industry under the auspices of the Industrial Welfare Association, of which he was president. The overall aim of the organization was to persuade Britain's industrial overlords to become more actively conscious of the need to improve working conditions for employees, to establish health centres and factory canteens, and to provide recreational facilities. As Sir John Wheeler-Bennett, Bertie's official biographer was to put it, 'Captains of Industry and Trade Union leaders became regular callers [on the Duke of York] ... and the Duke's influence made itself felt throughout the industrial life of Britain.' By their insistence to be allowed to do something useful, 'the Foreman' and the 'Factory Inspector', as Bertie and George were affectionately called by members of their family, proved that royalty could – and indeed wanted to be - more than ornamental baubles on the 'British Establishment' tree.

In his work for the Home Office Prince George was a popular and conscientious member of the Factory Inspectorate. More to the point, he was of value both to his department and to those whose working conditions it was his responsibility to review. Like Bertie, Prince George was adamant that he should be allowed to do his job without ceremony; employers were never to be given advance warning of his identity in order to avoid factories being smartened up and unwanted reception committees organized. In short, if his work was to be effective, George wanted to do it as anonymously as the rest of his Home Office colleagues. For the most part, that is exactly how it was; but it would be foolish to suggest that he was never recognized. Even at a time that knew nothing of the kind of technology and mass communication we take so much for granted, Prince George and his brothers were popular public figures whose photographs regularly graced newspapers and magazines. If, however, the Prince of Wales was generally considered the best-looking and most charismatic of George V's sons, a royal matinée idol adored by millions throughout the empire, George was a very close second. Physically the younger prince was somewhat taller than his brother and dark where the elder prince was fair. Both had blue eyes, though George's were of a deeper hue; and where David's voice was comparatively strong, with a slight inflection often likened to Cockney, George's was fey and almost feminine. Towards the end of his life David's features, in certain moods, assumed the look of his Hanoverian forebears, whereas Prince George, particularly in the set of his eyes and mouth, had always resembled the features of Britain's four Georges that continue to stare out at us out from court portraits by the likes of Zoffany, Gainsborough, Ramsay and Jean-Étienne Liotard.

After Prince George left the Royal Navy, he and the Prince of Wales became ever closer. They even shared the same house. Like his great-great uncle King William IV, who called it a white elephant and might easily have sold it to the highest bidder, David had never liked Buckingham Palace, and during the mid-1920s had been delighted when his father agreed to his setting up home at York House, St James's Palace. Once the official residence of George V and Queen Mary, York House is part of the rambling red-brick Tudor palace that Henry VIII built for his second queen, Anne Boleyn. It stands on the site of the 12th century hospital of St James the Less, which at that time was a home for 'leprous maidens'.

Having George share York House away from the censorious eye of their father, was a great pleasure to the Prince of Wales and between them they lived life to the full. David, fond of flying, steeple-chasing, hunting, shooting and golf, was as much at home in the company of sportsmen as he was in London's most fashionable night clubs perfecting the latest dances with his successive mistresses, Mrs Dudley Ward, Thelma, Viscountess Furness, and ultimately the twice-married American, Mrs Ernest Simpson whose name the entire world would soon come to know. Prince George shared his brother's passion for flying, but not for shooting. George preferred sailing and skiing. His love of night life, however, was every bit as strong as David's. With him on the dance floor at night spots, at private parties and at other social get togethers was the vivacious Lady Alexandra Curzon. Named after her godmother Queen Alexandra, but otherwise known as Baba, she was a daughter of the Marquess Curzon, former viceroy of India. In fact she and George became so close that there was talk among their friends and in the press of a possible marriage. Nothing came of it and when Baba, though she always remained very fond of the prince, married Edward 'Fruity' Metcalfe, a captain in the Indian cavalry and a friend of the Prince of Wales, in 1925, George was deeply upset.

That said, however, it wasn't long before George's passions were re-ignited, this time by banking-heiress and fun-loving débutante Poppy Baring. Duff Cooper, later 1st Viscount Norwich, watched closely as events between them unfolded and on 8 January 1927, he found 'Poppy sleeping peacefully in the arms of Prince George'. Six days later, he noted that there was 'talk of marriage', although Poppy herself said 'she couldn't bear the Royal Family' and to George's amusement, often made jokes about them. At the end of the month, with his customary love of speed, the prince rushed off to tell his parents that he wanted to marry Poppy. According to Duff Cooper, the king and queen took it 'wonderfully and raised hardly an objection ...' but then, only ten days later, it was all off. For reasons he either didn't know or was too discreet to divulge, Duff Cooper wrote,

'Unfavourable reports about poor Poppy appear to have reached His Majesty's ears, so the girl's sunk.'

For Prince George, like many other aristocratic young men, 'stage door johnnies' as many of them became known, the lure of the theatre and particularly of showgirls, was intoxicating. At a time when the general rule was that you could sleep with anyone who didn't threaten your position or your career and when showgirls were looked down upon, actresses so often fitted the bill. Certainly George's taste in women, both before and after his marriage, recognized no boundaries. Indeed, the African-American singer, dancer and comedienne Florence Mills whom George had first met in London in 1926 during the hit run of *Blackbirds*, one of Charles B. Cochran's revues, became one of his mistresses; while the movie stars Lois Sturt, Gloria Swanson and Talullah Bankhead also crossed his path.

For those who could afford it, jazz-age London in the 1920s was the place to be. It was an exciting post-war world and George and his brother David were in the thick of it together. The jazz musician Tiny Winters, who often saw the princes together at fashionable West End night spots such as Quaglino's and the Embassy Club, recalled one occasion when they stayed on all night at the latter venue. The moment they left, said Winters, the band 'shot out to catch the buses', and as they did so, ran into the royal brothers, who had 'just got out into the street, and one of them got [the other's] top hat [this was a time when silk toppers, white tie and tails were worn] and climbed up a lamp-post and stuck [it] on the iron bar .... Then the other one climbed up and got it. After that they were chasing one another, grabbing their top hats and kicking them about all over the street.'

Not all Prince George's activities were as knock-about or innocent. At the end of the 1920s, Alice Gwynne, who was far better known as Kiki Whitney Preston, a beautiful if wild American socialite and prominent member of Kenya's louche Happy Valley set, composed very largely of hedonistic aristocrats and adventurers, introduced Prince George to heroin, cocaine and morphine. Because of her own drug addiction Kiki, whose lovers also included Rudolf Valentino and Jorge Ferrara, the bisexual son of the Argentinian ambassador to London, with whom she and Prince George reportedly shared a *ménage à trios*, earned for herself the nickname 'the girl with the silver syringe'. Said to have miscarried a child that it was speculated may have been fathered by Prince George, Kiki was confronted by the Prince of Wales and persuaded to leave England. In the meantime, the prince took it upon himself to oversee his brother's recovery from drug addiction. Installed in a quiet country location and attended by qualified nursing staff as well as the Prince of Wales himself, George's painful rehabilitation took some time.

On one occasion, David wrote to his then mistress, Freda Dudley Ward, 'The cure has reached a rather tricky stage … I'm carrying out the work of doctor, jailer and detective combined. The old saying 'Boys will be boys' is alright until you get too old and should know the form better. He seems to lack all sense of knowing what is so obviously the wrong thing to do.'

Then as now, the rich and the high-born, with time on their hands, like-minded company and money to burn, were among those who thought little of experimenting with drugs. But that the king's son should have been one of them and should have become seriously addicted, revealed an unfortunate flaw in Prince George's character. Drugs, however, were not his only weakness. He was also promiscuous, self-indulgent and over-sexed; a man whom it was said at the time, 'would not be safe in a taxi with anyone of either sex.'

As a result of his sexual adventures, questions of paternity would be raised on more than one occasion. Indeed, if Kiki Whitney Preston had miscarried George's child another of his conquests, as author and journalist Christopher Wilson revealed in a newspaper article published in July 2013, did have a child who survived into adulthood. Violet Evans the daughter of a wealthy Canadian coal merchant was the sister of one of George's friends from his naval college days. And it was through her brother William that Violet met and became involved with Prince George. In 1926, she gave birth to a son who was adopted by the American-born, London-based book publisher, Cass Canfield, and renamed Michael Temple Canfield. In April 1953, at the age of twenty-seven, he married his first wife Lee Bouvier, younger sister of Jacqueline Kennedy Onassis. After they were divorced, Canfield married British aristocrat Laura Charteris, the ex-wife of both the 2nd Viscount Long and the 3rd earl of Dudley, and the future wife of the 10th Duke of Marlborough. On one occasion after they married in 1960, Laura and Michael lunched with Prince George's brother David and his wife, by now Duke and Duchess of Windsor. In her autobiography *Laughter from a Cloud*, Laura recalled how over that lunch, 'The Duke never stopped staring at Michael. So much so that I asked: "Is anything the matter?" The Duke quietly replied: "Yes. I am certain your husband is my brother's son". Another similar claim would one day be made by the novelist Barbara Cartland, who maintained that Prince George was the biological father of her daughter Raine McCorquodale, who as Countess Spencer would become step-mother to Diana, Princess of Wales.

Throughout his adult life, George's physical attraction to women was matched by an equally strong attraction to his own sex, with a particular penchant for the blond good looks of German boys. Back then, however, gay sex between men was illegal and dangerous. In fact, until the law was first changed some forty years later, homosexual activity was punishable by imprisonment and in some parts of the world even by death. It was therefore fortunate for George that his position would afford him greater protection from prosecution, though not from the ability to jeopardize his own reputation as well as that of the monarchy itself. That threat became a reality when by the end of the 1920s George's careless indiscretions meant he started leaving compromising evidence of his homosexuality.

It is a known fact that on just one occasion Buckingham Palace had to send two 'emissaries' to Paris where, acting on behalf of the king, they burgled the apartment of one of George's boyfriends in order to retrieve a gold box with a personal inscription on the lid, together with a number of highly personal and incriminating letters. Anthony Blunt, a third cousin of Queen Elizabeth (the Queen Mother), one-time Surveyor of the King's (and later the Queen's) Pictures, and soviet spy (he was unmasked as the 'fourth man' in the infamous Cambridge spy ring that included Kim Philby, Guy Burgess and Donald Maclean), was on the list of George's putative lovers, as was Prince Louis Ferdinand of Prussia, who described George as 'artistic and effeminate and used a strong perfume.' It was a description that not only chimed with George's liking for dressing up, but also with the story of a visit he made backstage at the Phoenix Theatre after a performance of the 1930 comedy *Private Lives*. The star of the show was the celebrated Gertrude Lawrence who on returning to her dressing room was surprised and bemused to find Prince George sitting in front of her dressing table mirror trying on one of her wigs, complete with hair ornaments. It was another of George's penchants the public would know nothing about. Nor would the public know of the relationship George had with Noël Coward, the flamboyant author of *Private Lives,* who found international fame as a playwright, composer, director, actor, singer and wit. The 'Master' as Coward became known in the theatre world, described his liaison with Prince George as 'a little dalliance', and although Graham Payn, another of Coward's lovers, denied it was ever physical, Charles Russell, his New York representative, told the author Michael Thornton that 'Noël used to refer constantly to his affair with the Duke of Kent. He seemed rather proud of it and at times was almost a bore on the subject.' Adding fuel to the fire, it was reported at the time that the 'security services' were aware that Prince George and Noël Coward 'had been seen parading together through the streets of London, dressed and made up as women, and had once been arrested by the police ...' They were of course released when the true identity of the two 'ladies' was discovered.

Besides the more scandalous or at least the more salacious episodes that defined George's private life, there was also that aspect of his character, touched upon earlier, that cared deeply about things of beauty, from priceless works of art to interior decoration. As a bachelor prince, he received an official civil list allowance of £10,000 a year until he married. Then his tax-free income was increased to £25,000, in today's currency literally worth a King's ransom. Yet even on an annuity of £10,000, George accumulated a very fine collection of antique furniture, first-edition books, Georgian silver, porcelain, bibelots and pictures, including the famous 'Altieri' Claudes entitled *The Father of Psyche Sacrificing at the Temple of Apollo* and *Landscape with the Arrival of Aeneas before the City of Pallanteum,* by the French 17th-century landscape artist, Claude Lorrain, which were brought to England to great acclaim by the art collector William Beckford in 1799. Of Prince George's own prowess as a collector, the late Sir Oliver Millar (Surveyor of The Queen's Pictures 1972-88) said that he was 'the most distinguished royal connoisseur since George IV'.

CHAPTER EIGHT
DUKE AND DUCHESS
OF KENT

Until news of her engagement to Prince George was announced, Princess Marina was an unknown quantity. Royalty in exile rarely excited a great deal of attention, and the Greek royal family was no exception. Yet when Prince and Princess Nicholas accompanied their daughter and her fiancé back to Paris from Bohinj, Marina was no longer the unknown princess who (like many aristocratic women of modest means) had posed for publicity photographs to promote Pond's Cold Cream, had strolled in the Bois de Boulogne, fed the swans in the Tuileries Gardens or travelled around the city by public transport.

Suddenly, or so it seemed, everybody in Paris knew who she was and, just as suddenly, friends who had deserted the family when they were expelled from Greece sprang from nowhere to offer congratulations in the hope of rejoining Prince and Princess Nicholas's diminished circle. At the 10th arrondissement Gare du Nord (North Station), upon their arrival from Yugoslavia, the royal party was besieged by crowds eager to catch a glimpse of the prince and princess; while British and European reporters, barely restrained by a cordon of gendarmes, jostled with one another for quotes and photographs. Astounded though they were by such an unexpected welcome, Prince Nicholas is alleged to have been indignant at the sudden acknowledgement of his family's existence. 'Darling, what *does* it matter?' Marina is said to have asked her father. 'Would you expect people to behave otherwise?'

Within the next few weeks the British public knew all there was to know about Prince George's fiancée, all gathered from carefully prepared press releases, newspaper features and cinema newsreels. Even the princess herself yielded to media blandishments and gave interviews in her parents' apartment. During the 1930s, long before the proliferation of health warnings and social ostracism, the sight of public figures smoking cigarettes usually gave rise to little or no comment. But because she was a princess, Marina caused a minor stir when she was first seen smoking in public. The Duke of Windsor would sum up that kind of reaction, when he said, 'It has been my experience that the pleased incredulity with which the public reacts to the elementary demonstrations on the part of royalty that they are, after all, like other people, is matched by the public's firm refusal to accept them as such.'

On 12 September, leaving Marina in Paris to consult the British-born designer Edward Molyneux at his salon on the rue Royale about her wedding dress and trousseau, Prince George flew back to London. That same afternoon, before preparing to take the night train to Scotland, the prince chose the engagement ring he would give to his bride-to-be–a large square Kashmir sapphire, flanked on either side by baton (or oblong) diamonds, set in platinum. Following the custom in certain countries such as Greece, Russia and Germany, Princess Marina invariably wore her engagement and wedding rings not on the third finger of her left hand but on her right.

On Saturday 15 September, Prince George left Balmoral Castle, where he had joined the king and queen, to travel back to York House. The following day Marina and her parents arrived at Folkestone from France. The crowds of well wishers who waited to greet her, and the cheers of welcome, were later compared to the scenes that surrounded the arrival of her late great-aunt Alexandra of Denmark, Tennyson's 'Sea-King's daughter', when she arrived in England as the bride of the future Edward VII seventy-one years earlier in 1863. Feeling 'a little dazed', as she put it, Marina told reporters, 'I am so overwhelmed. I had not expected this wonderfully generous reception.' Folkestone's generosity was equalled at London's Victoria Station, where Prince George greeted his fiancée. Outside thousands gathered in the streets for a glimpse of the princess and, in a gesture of welcome, many women in the crowd threw handfuls of rose petals in front of the royal car as it slowly made its way to St James's Palace. There another throng awaited them, though this one, reluctant to disperse once the couple had stepped inside York House, began calling for them. In response to cries of 'We want Marina', the prince and princess appeared at an open window. As she waved, Marina's engagement ring caught the light. 'What stone is it?' came a voice from the crowd. 'It's a sapphire', the princess replied, moving her hand from side to side.

A few weeks later Prince George wrote to his close friend – and Marina's brother-in-law – Prince Paul of Yugoslavia, to thank him 'a million times' for his hospitality at Bohinj and 'for letting me see Marina and so get engaged to her'. The prince enthused, 'It's all so lovely and I am so happy that I can hardly believe it. Everyone is so delighted with her – the crowd especially – 'cos when she arrived at Victoria Station they expected a dowdy princess – such as unfortunately my family are – but when they saw this lovely chic creature – they could hardly believe it and even the men were interested and shouted "Don't change – don't let them change you!" Of course she won't be changed – not if I have anything to do with it. My parents were charming and so pleased with M and me!'

Since the 1850s, when the Prince Consort bought the estate as a private retreat, Balmoral has always had a very particular place in the affections of successive generations of the royal family. 'This Dear Paradise' is how Queen Victoria, the castle's very first chatelaine, described it. And it was at Balmoral, from where George V had formally announced his son's engagement, that Princess Marina, together with Prince and Princess Nicholas, spent the week that followed their arrival in Britain. One traditional event held during the royal family's traditional late summer holiday at Balmoral was (and still is) the ghillies' ball. During Marina's first visit, it was held in the pine-panelled ballroom on the evening of 19 September. Preceded by the skirl of the bagpipes provided by seven pipers, the king and queen led Prince George and Princess Marina, the Duke and Duchess of York, and Prince and Princess Arthur of Connaught to the recessed mirrored royal dais. There the king – who no longer danced – settled himself next to the archbishop of Canterbury, Dr Cosmo Gordon Lang, to enjoy the scene. The programme that night, as at every ghillies' ball since 1919, featured twelve dances; among them a Paul Jones, The Dashing White Sergeant, the Circassian Circle, Spanish Gavotte and Flirtation Polka. In honour of Princess Marina, who had taken lessons from Queen Mary, and who danced every dance, a Greek national air was included in the selection of music. 'I was enchanted [by] the ghillies' ball,' Marina told friends afterwards. 'There the servants dance with the royal family without any sense of familiarity, but with the utmost good friendship.'

Two days later it was announced that the wedding of Prince George and Princess Marina would take place at Westminster Abbey on the morning of Thursday 29 November, and that the Anglican ceremony would be followed by another, this time according to the rites of the Greek Orthodox Church, of which the princess would remain a lifelong member, in the private chapel at Buckingham Palace. *The Times* reminded its readers: 'A precedent for the holding of a second service at a royal marriage is provided by the wedding of the late Duke of Edinburgh [Queen Victoria's second son, Alfred] ... to the late Grand Duchess Marie Alexandrovna of Russia [daughter of Tsar Alexander II] on January 23, 1874, in the Winter Palace at St Petersburg. On that occasion ... the bride and bridegroom were first married according to the Greek [sic] rite in the Imperial Chapel, and again, immediately afterwards, in accordance with the Church of England Service, read in the Alexander Hall by the Dean of Westminster ....'

On 24 September Prince George and Princess Marina returned to London from Scotland, travelling by overnight sleeper. Arriving at King's Cross Station just before 7.30am, the royal party looked out on a platform crowded with Londoners who, despite the hour, were waiting to cheer them. From the station George drove Marina to Claridge's, where she and her parents occupied one of the elegant second-floor suites. Then the prince went home to York House, but not before arranging to have a box each of pink roses and pink lilies delivered to his fiancée.

Shortly after midday, George was back at the hotel to lunch with Marina, her parents and the Infanta Beatrice of Spain, after which the prince took his bride to visit Cartier the jewellers, to shop for personal gifts. Cartier was, in fact, one of Prince George's favourite haunts and when, four years later, he was appointed governor-general designate of Australia, Chips Channon, diarist, MP and one of the prince's most intimate friends, wryly commented that George's posting 'would save him £500,000 or more, the money he would certainly have spent in London shops.'

In celebration of his fourth son's marriage, the King announced his intention of reviving a royal title that had died with Queen Victoria's father

114 years before. In April 1799 King George III, great-great-grandfather of George V, created his own fourth son, Edward, Duke of Kent and Strathearn and earl of Dublin. When the duke died twenty-one years later, leaving his German-born widow Viktoria Luise with an eight-month-old daughter, the future Queen Victoria, his titles fell into abeyance. Now George V had decided to create the dukedom anew and on 12 October 1934, Prince George became Duke of Kent, earl of St Andrews and baron Downpatrick.

By then Princess Marina and her parents had returned temporarily to Paris. But before they left, she issued a statement which not only touched upon the seriousness of inter-war unemployment and poverty in the United Kingdom (only the year before unemployment had stood at 3,000,000 or 20% of the working population), but also spoke of her personal sympathy with those most directly concerned. 'I would like the people of England to share in some way my great happiness on the occasion of my engagement to Prince George' she said. 'As you know, my years of exile have taught me how much unhappiness there is in the world. Although I should be happy to think that the preparations for my wedding were in some small measure giving employment to those who need it, I should be more than happy for the unemployed, and particularly for their children, to receive any money which has been intended for the purchase of wedding gifts for me.'

Princess Marina's regard for the poor of Britain served to increase her popularity still further. Yet while many cities and towns did send wedding presents, others responded to the princess's appeal and put official funds to more practical and beneficial use.

On 9 October, however, one event had occurred that not only subdued the celebratory mood surrounding plans for the royal wedding, but briefly threatened its postponement. That day, less than an hour after he had stepped ashore in Marseilles to be greeted by the French Foreign Minister Louis Barthou, at the start of a state visit to France, intended to strengthen the alliance between the two countries, King Alexander of Yugoslavia was shot and killed by a Croatian revolutionary, Vlado Chernozemski. Presciently, on the night before he set out for France, Princess Paul – Marina's sister Olga – had urged Alexander to wear a bullet-proof vest, but her pleas had been dismissed.

In his will the king appointed his cousin Prince Paul along with Ivan Perović, Governor of Croatia, and Radenko Stanković, Professor of Medicine at Belgrade University, and a man who had won the monarch's confidence, to rule until his eleven-year-old son Peter II attained his majority in September 1941. Of the three Prince Paul was nominated first regent. The funeral of the assassinated king took place in Belgrade on 14 October and Princess Marina together with the new Duke of Kent, who acted as official representative of George V and the British people, were among the mourners.

In the event, the royal wedding was not postponed, but in the weeks that led up to it, the Prince of Wales seemed somehow to be nursing a sorrow of his own; the imminent loss of his favourite brother and close friend. Of that time, the Duchess of Windsor would write, 'As I watched the Prince ... it seemed to me that a sadness began to envelop him. He and his younger brother were very close, and the bonds of blood were strengthened by an unusual kinship of spirit .... Before his wedding, Prince George was at [Fort Belvedere] almost every weekend. I rather suspected that the Prince, who was to be best man ... thought it was just as well to keep a close eye on the bridegroom-to-be until he had been safely led to the altar'.

If, however, the Prince of Wales was to lose 'the only powerful male relationship he had ever known in his life', as the late Audrey Whiting, royal correspondent and respected journalist, put it, he was about to win the most powerful relationship he was to know with a woman. That year, he and Wallis Simpson had taken a private holiday cruise aboard Lord Moyne's yacht *Rosaura*, and it was then, in Wallis's own words, that she and the prince 'crossed the line that marks the indefinable boundary between friendship and love'.

For the time being, while nobody had the remotest inkling of the crisis David and Wallis' relationship would cause, the only love story all Europe was interested in was that of George and Marina, or 'that dazzling pair' as Chips Channon referred to them. By the third week of November London was *en fête* and waiting for *the* royal event of 1934. Princess Marina was back from Paris and, with Prince and Princess Nicholas, staying at Buckingham Palace as the guest of the king and queen. On 27 November, a sumptuous pre-wedding ball for more than 2,000 guests was held there in honour of the bridal couple, while in the West End crowds of sightseers marvelled at the brilliance and ingenuity of the street decorations. Bond Street, in particular, had pulled out all the stops, and its entire length from Piccadilly to Oxford Street was hung with garlands of waxed-paper flowers, forming brightly coloured arches, from which were suspended hundreds of Greek and British flags. Wedding bells, entwined monograms, and portraits of bride and groom were displayed in nearly every shop window, while coloured lights and festive streamers heightened the carnival-like atmosphere.

In the state rooms at St James's Palace the last of the exhibits were being put in place before the wedding presents went on public display in aid of charity. Among the gifts silver and furniture predominated. The Lord Mayor and Citizens of the City of London, for example, gave a silver dinner service, while the Corporation of the City of London gave a set of 18th-century silver tureens and plate. The Prime Minister and the Cabinet gave a partner's desk in English walnut and British Honduras mahogany, and the twelve senior Livery Companies presented a set of six Queen Anne walnut chairs. Other gifts were chosen to appeal to the duke's particular taste. The Royal Academy gave a George III bracket clock; Tomáš Masaryk, the very first president of Czechoslovakia, sent a set of engraved glass, while President Albert Lebrun of France gave seven classical groups in Sèvres porcelain. From the Greek community in Cape Town, Princess Marina received a luxurious fan of eighteen ostrich feathers mounted in mother-of-pearl, while closer to home, the London antique furniture and art dealers Messrs M. Harris & Sons gave the couple a superb Chinese red and gold lacquered cabinet on an elaborate gilded base together with a six-panelled Chinese screen. The jewellers Boucheron and Cartier respectively gave a jade and diamond cigarette box and pigskin toilet case that was specially designed for Prince George.

Among the most magnificent gifts Princess Marina received were family jewels; an entire suite of sapphires and diamonds – tiara, necklace, brooches and earrings – from Queen Mary, and a diamond and pearl sautoir from the king and queen together. There was a pearl and diamond scroll tiara and a large diamond bow brooch from Marina's mother, and from the bridegroom himself, a ruby and diamond bracelet, and an antique necklace of 372 pearls with diamond motifs.

On the day before the wedding Bertie and Elizabeth, the Duke and Duchess of York, gave a lunch party for the couple at their house at 145 Piccadilly, and that evening George and Marina were accompanied by Queen Mary when they attended a performance of *Theatre Royal*, at the Lyric Theatre in Shaftesbury Avenue. Such was the public's response that, as *The Times* reported, 'The Duke and the Princess were given a tumultuous ovation when the royal cars arrived at Piccadilly Circus. The large crowd swarmed round and cheered wildly. The escort of police cars and the police on duty had difficulty in clearing a way'.

Royal wedding day, Thursday 29 November, was all the weather forecasters said it would be: a typically grey, damp, misty winter's day without so much as a hint of sunshine. Indeed, the street lamps were still burning at midday. Nevertheless, crowds still thronged the royal route from Buckingham Palace to Westminster Abbey and back, people hung from every available window and rooftop, and the huge red and blue stands in Parliament Square had started to fill with spectators well before dawn. The bells of the abbey began ringing a full peal of more than 5,000 changes as soon as the first guests began to arrive; road surfaces were sanded to prevent the horses from slipping; street vendors sold all manner of souvenirs and favours; and the boys of Westminster School, traditional cheerleaders on occasions such as this, took up their specially appointed places near the abbey's great West Door. Beneath the bare plane trees and the bunting and flags, troops and military bands lining the streets were marshalled into position, while behind them discreet plainclothes police officers kept a watch on the crowds.

At Buckingham Palace, in the white and gold Ball-Supper Room where the wedding breakfast was to be held, florists completed their arrangements of roses, carnations, chrysanthemums, heather and lily-of-the-valley, while the wedding cake was carefully set up on a table of its own. Topped with a trailing bouquet of roses, orange blossom and snowdrops, the four-tier confection – more a pseudo-gothic work of art decorated with bells, cupids and the couple's entwined initials– stood nine feet tall and weighed 800 pounds.

Amid all the pomp and splendour, one small incident added an everyday dimension to the occasion. Shortly before he put on his gold-fringed ceremonial naval uniform, his Garter ribbon, stars and sword, George, Duke of Kent discovered that he had almost no money in his wallet. So, slipping out of York House he walked unrecognized to his bank to cash a cheque.

'Surely you could have sent someone else,' said an incredulous Prince of Wales, when his brother reappeared.

'Oh, easily,' George replied, 'but it gave me something to do.'

By 10.30 that morning, the 2,000 guests had taken their seats inside Westminster Abbey ahead of the arrival of the royal family. First among them was the bridegroom's sister Mary, the Princess Royal, with the Duchess of York and her four-year-old daughter Margaret Rose, together with a number of more junior-ranking members of the family, among them Queen Victoria's granddaughters Princess Alice, Countess of Athlone, and Lady Patricia Ramsay who as Princess Patricia of Connaught had unwittingly established the trend for royal weddings at the abbey after she was married there in 1919. The bride's sisters, Olga and Elizabeth, were also among the first arrivals, followed by George V and Queen Mary, Princess Nicholas and the kings and queens of Norway, Denmark and Greece, and Olga's husband Paul, as Regent of Yugsolavia. Before the bride herself, the last members of the royal family to arrive were the Duke of Kent with his brothers the Prince of Wales and the Duke of York.

Finally, having travelled in a state landau in its claret, gold and scarlet livery, the royal coat of arms emblazoned on its doors, and accompanied by a Captain's Escort of the Life Guards, Princess Marina made her entrance to the sound of a welcoming fanfare played by the State Trumpeters from the bridge of the organ screen that spanned the nave of the ancient abbey church. Waiting for her were her eight bridesmaids. Dressed in white and silver, the six older attendants, five of them princesses, were Eugenie, Irene and Katherine of Greece, Juliana of the Netherlands, Kyra of Russia, and the Lady Iris Mountbatten. The two youngest, wearing short skirts of stiffened white tulle, so that the King could see 'their pretty little knees', were Princess Elizabeth of York, the future Queen Elizabeth II, and Lady Mary Cambridge.

Dressed by the Paris-based, British couturier Edward Molyneux, who also designed for Greta Garbo, Gertrude Lawrence and Vivien Leigh, Princess Marina shimmered in a dress of silver and white brocaded lamé, patterned with English roses, which had been made by a team of seamstresses who, at Marina's request, included Russian émigrées. A twelve-foot court train lined in silver fell from her shoulders, while her tulle veil was secured by a diamond fringe tiara which the City of London had given to her as a wedding present. Pinned to her left shoulder, Marina also wore the Family Order which George V had given to her as a personal gift and which consisted of an oval miniature of the king surrounded by diamonds and fastened by a diamond crown to a bow of pale blue watered silk. (Almost without exception, the exclusive Family Order was (and continues to be) given by each Sovereign only to female members of the royal family).

Having walked to the steps of the high altar on the arm of her father Prince Nicholas, to the processional hymn *Gracious Spirit, Holy Ghost* by Sir John Stainer, the marriage ceremony was opened by the dean of Westminster and conducted by the Archbishop of Canterbury. 'George Edward Alexander Edmund,' Dr Lang intoned, 'wilt though have this woman to thy wedded wife, to live together after God's ordinance in the holy estate of matrimony ... and forsaking all other, keep thee only unto her, so long as ye both shall live?'

'I will,' responded the duke.

Then the archbishop turned to the bride with the very same charge: 'Marina, wilt thou have this man to thy wedded husband ...?'

'I will,' she replied softly but firmly.

'Who giveth this woman to be married to this man?' archbishop Lang then asked and Prince Nicholas gave Marina's hand to the primate. At that point, as George and Marina were to take their vows, the Prince of Wales, as best man (or 'supporter' in courtly language) should have produced the ring to be blessed. But when his mother glanced at him, David seemed to be miles away. Queen Mary touched her husband's arm and unobtrusively the king signalled to his son. Immediately the prince took the ring from his pocket and placed it on the archbishop's open prayer book.

At the end of the Church of England service, the new Duchess of Kent and her husband processed from Westminster Abbey to the bridal march from *Lohengrin*, otherwise known as 'Here comes the Bride', followed by Mendelssohn's Wedding March. Outside the bells pealed and the crowds roared their greetings. On their way back to Buckingham Palace, the Glass Coach in which George and Marina travelled, slowly passed St George's Hospital (now the 5-star Lanesborough Hotel) at Hyde Park

Corner, where nursing staff and some of the patients waited to see them. It was a special moment for the Duke of Kent, not only because he was president of the hospital, but because, at his request, the nation's wedding present took the form of a large donation to the hospital's rebuilding fund.

With their return to Buckingham Palace, George and Marina made their way beneath the columned porte-cochère of the Grand Entrance and across the white, red and gold Grand Hall to the private chapel. There in a half-hour service conducted almost entirely in Greek by the Metropolitan Germanos Thyateira, Exarch of the Ecumenical Patriarchate in Western Europe, and the Great Archimandrite Michael Constantinidis, they were married according to the rites of the Greek Orthodox Church. Later that afternoon, in the gathering dusk of that damp November day, after they had sat down to a wedding breakfast of *Filet de sole, Côtes d'agneau braisées, Perdreaux à la crème, Pêches Melba* and *Corbeilles de friandises,* the Duke and Duchess of Kent climbed into an open landau and, chased by members of their families throwing rose petals and tiny silver horseshoes, drove off through Hyde Park towards Paddington Station at the start of their honeymoon which began modestly enough at Himley Hall, the earl of Dudley's estate in Staffordshire and Trent Park, the country home of Sir Philip Sassoon in Barnet. Not for them, however, the three days at Windsor Castle the young Queen Victoria and Prince Albert had had, or the mere three weeks George's elder brother Bertie, Duke of York and his bride had enjoyed in Surrey, Glamis and Windsor, but an altogether more indulgent five-month holiday that culminated in a 12-week cruise of the West Indies. Popular though George and Marina were, such blatant extravagance stretched the goodwill of vast numbers of everyday men and women struggling to make ends meet. Nor, though for quite another reason, did the marriage resonate in full measure with the people of Marina's homeland. Writing to President Roosevelt, the American diplomat Lincoln McVeagh said, 'You will have seen a lot in the American papers about the marriage of Princess Marina of Greece to the Duke of Kent. There is some sentiment, or sentimentality, about that here too. But almost fifty per cent of the population of Greece would emphasize to any inquirer that the princess has no Greek blood and no Greek passport.... Royalist propaganda is noticeably absent.'

CHAPTER NINE
PRIVATE LIVES

It was, coincidentally, while they were on honeymoon in the Caribbean in March 1935 that George and Marina first met America's thirty-second president in person. Then in his second year in office, Franklin D. Roosevelt was visiting Nassau aboard Vincent Astor's yacht *Nourmahal*. Perhaps because his curiosity had been aroused by Lincoln McVeagh's letter, or simply because they happened to be in the same place at the same time, the president invited the duke and duchess to lunch with him.

To many Americans at that time who seemed to think that Britain and the British had not progressed much beyond gas lighting and horse-drawn omnibuses, the general concept of royalty was no more advanced. Nevertheless, if President Roosevelt had expected George and Marina to be courteous visitors from an antediluvian world, he was to be pleasantly surprised. In them he found spontaneity coupled with intellect and an unaffected charm; qualities which he considered highly attractive. Equally, if little more than diplomatic niceties on their part had led the duke and duchess to accept the president's invitation they, too, were to be captivated. Almost from the moment they met on 27 March, a cordial friendship was established; so much so that when they parted later that afternoon, there was no doubting the sincerity of the president's invitation to 'come and see me in Washington'. So taken were the duke and duchess for their part that the same evening Prince George cabled Roosevelt aboard the *Nourmahal*, 'My wife and I will always retain the happiest memories of our delightful, informal, meeting today. We both wish you health, happiness and a successful administration and look forward to seeing you again in the near future.'

The Kents' protracted honeymoon finally came to an end when they arrived back in London on 14 April and drove to Windsor where they stayed for a few days before moving into their new home. Number 3 Belgrave Square was one of the tall, uniformly white, terraced houses that the famous 19th-century builder and architect, Thomas Cubitt, built around a central garden for the 2nd Earl Grosvenor in the 1820s. A century later, number 3 was owned by Lady Juliet Duff, daughter of the celebrated Marchioness of Ripon, famous for dazzling 'every London drawing-room' with 'her wit, good looks and energy'; and it was Lady Juliet who leased the house to the duke and duchess with the generous provision that they could redecorate and refurbish as they wished. For Prince George, with his instinctive flair for interior decoration, the temptation to make changes was irresistible. 'His sense of decorative values,' James Wentworth-Day wrote, 'was so sure that he could order silks, brocades, chintzes and colours with an eye and appreciation of a woman.' Even Marina had to admit that she left everything to her husband's judgement. Mabell, Countess of Airlie recalled, 'In the 1930s I often dined at the Duke and Duchess of Kent's house in Belgrave Square, and I was always impressed not so much by the externals of happiness – the brilliance of the conversation, the beauti-fully arranged rooms and the perfectly chosen meal – as by the deeper harmony of two temperaments.

'Once when I complimented the Duchess on the dinner she laughed. 'I am really a very bad hostess. I must confess that I didn't know what we were going to eat tonight until the food appeared. My husband chose the dinner and the wine – and the flowers and everything else. He enjoys doing it, and so I always leave the household affairs to him. I let him make all the decisions over furniture and decorations. He has a wonderful sense of colour and design.'

For a woman like Marina, who was far from submissive by nature, taking a back seat in this way was a very considerable compliment to the talents of her husband. Before long George had devised new colour schemes for most of the rooms, using a wide range of skilfully blended pastel shades, both to enhance the period and contemporary furnishings and to act as a subtle backdrop to his collection of pictures and *objets d'art*. The house was not without its more dramatic touches, however, and it has been said that, in keeping with the 'assertively modern style' as his-torian Bevis Hillier described the prevalent art deco look, Marina's own bathroom was decorated in black and silver, a variation on Juliet Duff's original theme of black and gold, while her bedroom featured a full-length mirrored alcove and neo-classical *Directoire* bed beneath a striped canopy of peach and green.

While Prince George was the 'master planner' of the pair, Princess Marina was not without her likes and dislikes. Indeed, by casually remarking that she would not care for her house 'to look like a bar', she unwittingly dampened the popular trend for chrome furniture and what were described as 'razzle-dazzle' cushions and curtains. Of more significance was the influence she had on women's fashion and lifestyle. Always noted for her elegance, she started a craze for small pillbox hats and turbans – with or without the addition of feathers and net veiling, and like the present Princess Royal during the early 1970s, also created a vogue for wide-brimmed hats. 'Marina blue' was a shade named in her honour; her hairstyles were copied, and – or so it was said – women took up smoking, simply because it became known that Marina smoked. She was responsible for helping to make trousers acceptable among 'respectable' women (something that had previously been considered a fashion taboo), and she did everything to revive a sustainable interest in cotton. 'When she first came to England,' one unnamed textile manufacturer was quoted as saying at the time, 'no really smart woman would have worn a cotton dress, but the duke told her of the depression in Lancashire and the desperate poverty of many of the people. She asked her dressmaker to design cotton frocks for her and wore them ... until the fashion was firmly established.'

Princess Marina's interest in clothes and her own ability as a needlewoman had originally surfaced many years before in Paris, when she would make dresses to her own design. According to Jennifer Ellis, writing in the early 1950s, the duchess had three secrets for successful dressing: 'She never lets herself be influenced by the fact that something is the latest style, if she does not think it would suit her. She never minds being seen in the same dress several times. And she always chooses clothes that are interchangeable. In her wardrobe no hat goes with just one pair of shoes and no other, and most of her scarves and stoles have reversible linings.'

Later, during the Second World War, when clothing coupons ruled out even the smallest extravagance, Marina's resourcefulness and versatility were said to have led her to make several summer dresses 'from material which had been bought before the war for curtains'.

One of the greatest tributes to the princess's sense of style was made by the late couturier John Cavanagh, who not only created many of her most successful outfits, but who would also design the wedding dresses of her daughter-in-law, Katharine Worsley, when she married the present Duke of Kent in 1961, and of her daughter Alexandra when she married two years later.

'To me,' Cavanagh, who had begun his career under Edward Molyneux in Paris, told the present writer, [Princess Marina] was sheer magic ... personifying superb elegance. Later she was often my inspiration. She was, from the word go, the woman I wanted to dress more than any other in the world.'

While style and elegance were inherent in Princess Marina as in no other British royal lady at that time, one aspect of her 'look' jarred with her mother-in-law. Quite early on Queen Mary made it known that George V did not like Marina painting her fingernails. 'Your George might not like it,' the princess retorted, 'but mine does!' The subject was never mentioned again.

It was at 3 Belgrave Square on 9 October 1935 that the Duchess of Kent gave birth to the first of her three children. By the time she and George had returned from their honeymoon Marina was already three months pregnant and, when it came to redecorating their new home, the duke, perhaps anticipating the birth of a son, chose a blue and white colour scheme for the top-floor nursery.

At the beginning of October, Marina's parents came to London for the birth of their first Kent grandchild, whose arrival was then expected on the sixteenth of the month. Among Prince and Princess Nicholas's first visitors was Chips Channon, George and Marina's neighbour in Belgrave Square. On 7 October, he noted in his diary, 'I went to Claridge's to have tea with the Nicholases of Greece. The Duchess of Kent was there in a brown dress and much bejewelled, and rather large.... She was sweetness itself, but she has not become in the least English.... At one point the Grand Duchess [Princess Nicholas] sent her daughter into the next room to fetch her spectacles and the Duchess went meekly. She has been well brought up in an old-fashioned, affectionate way.'

Channon, who also had a keen eye for the men and in his own words found the Duke of Kent 'altogether irresistible', followed Marina's pregnancy with great interest, partly out of friendship and partly because his own wife, the former Lady Honor Guinness, was expecting their first, and only, child at much the same time. In the event, and to Channon's uncontrollable delight, both Marina and Honor gave birth on the very same day.

On the evening of 8 October, when it became clear that the duchess's baby would be born at any time, Fleet Street, then home to England's national newspaper industry, despatched reporters and photographers to 3 Belgrave Square, where they all assembled in one of the ground floor rooms. Shortly before midnight the Duke of Kent put his head round the door. 'I just thought I'd tell you that some hot coffee is being sent in to you,' he said. 'After that I'm afraid the kitchens will be closed, but there'll be someone on duty just after six who will get you some breakfast.' Then he added, 'I do hope it'll be over soon. I don't think I could stand much more of this.'

The newsmen didn't have to wait for breakfast. At 2.15am Princess Marina gave birth to a son. Edward George Nicholas Paul Patrick, as the boy was christened at Buckingham Palace on 20 November, was King George and Queen Mary's fifth grandchild and, to add to their pleasure, he was born in what was an especially memorable year for the royal family.

At St Paul's Cathedral on 6 May the nation had celebrated the silver jubilee of George V's reign. An occasion of the greatest pomp and ceremony, it was one in which Marina was again singled out by the press for the elegance of her creamy-fawn outfit and vast wide-brimmed, ostrich feather adorned hat. Later, just a month after the birth of Prince Edward of Kent, yet another royal occasion caught the nation's imagination. This time it was the wedding at Buckingham Palace on 6 November, of George's brother, Prince Henry, Duke of Gloucester, and Lady Alice Montagu-Douglas-Scott, daughter of the seventh Duke of Buccleuch who, like her new sister-in-law, Elizabeth, Duchess of York, was the scion of a noble Scottish house. Like George and Marina, Harry and Alice were to have been married at Westminster Abbey, but the death from cancer of the bride's father, just eighteen days before, and the king's own fragile health, meant a change of plan and a change of venue. Unlike George and Marina, there was to be no prolonged and self-indulgent honeymoon. As the new Duchess of Gloucester would one day write in her memoirs, 'The Duke of Kent's recent honeymoon had been considered too extravagant, so we were told to spend ours quietly in England.' Within the space of six months the king had celebrated his silver jubilee, the birth of his third grandson, and the marriage of his third son. But the happiness each of those events had brought him was marred by the death of his favourite sister Princess Victoria.

Born on 6 July 1868, 'Toria' was the second of Edward VII's three daughters and the only one of them not to have married. That she was to die an embittered spinster was due entirely to the fact that her mother, Queen Alexandra, kept her at home to act as her companion. Yet Toria, who ached for romance and love, was not without her suitors. Among them was the widowed and considerably older, Lord Rosebery. Another was the again much older Admiral Lord Fisher, who was to write of her in her early middle age, 'Princess Victoria, who used to be scraggy, lanky and anaemic, has developed into an opulent figure with a rosy, plump face! She looked very handsome and I told her so, and her tall figure makes her most imposing now.'

As a result of being cast in the role of unmarried daughter, shuffling with her mother between Marlborough House in London and Sandringham in Norfolk, Princess Victoria grew old before her time, becoming vaguely eccentric and seeking solace in ill health, real and imagined. When Queen Alexandra died in 1925, Toria, by now aged fifty-seven, went – for the very first time in her life - in search of a home of her own. She found what she was looking for in a mid-Victorian, multi-gabled house, north of the village of Iver in Buckinghamshire, called The Coppins. The prefix was eventually dropped and the house became known simply as 'Coppins'.

Lending structure, if not purpose, to the princess's otherwise lonely existence were the closeness of her relationship with her brother George V and the interest she took in village life. A familiar figure in Iver, where she played the part of 'Lady Bountiful' to perfection, including having become president of the Iver Horticultural Society, Toria would often visit the local school, but rarely if ever went inside. Instead, she would stand in the playground peering through the classroom windows, waving and calling to the children.

Almost every day Princess Victoria and her brother would speak on the telephone, and there is one story which, apart from being amusing, provides an insight into the very close bond she shared with the king. Having put through a call to him, the princess heard a click and shouted down the line, 'Is that you, you old bugger?' to which a startled palace telephonist replied, 'I'm sorry, your Royal Highness, his Majesty is not yet on the line.'

The shock of Princess Victoria's death on 3 December 1935, at the age of sixty-seven, is often said to have hastened the end of the king's own life. In failing health for some years, George V cancelled the State Opening of Parliament and shortly after Toria's funeral at Frogmore in the private Home Park at Windsor, retired to Sandringham. Shortly afterwards, the king made what was to be his final Christmas broadcast to the empire, planted a cedar tree in front of Sandringham House, rode his 'fat little shooting pony' around the estate and, as he wrote in his diary, 'saw my Kent grandson in his bath.' On 12 January the king, breathless, lethargic and feeling generally unwell, took to his bed. He died eight days later at 11.55pm on Monday, 20 January.

For five days the remains of King George V lay in state at Westminster Hall, the oldest surviving part of the Thames-side Palace of Westminster (otherwise known as the Houses of Parliament) in central London; and it was there at midnight on 27 January, the day before the king's funeral at Windsor, that the Duke of Kent and his three brothers, David, the new King Edward VIII, Bertie, Duke of York and Henry, Duke of Gloucester, paid a unique tribute to their father. Dressed in ceremonial uniform and with swords reversed and heads bowed, they replaced officers of the Household Brigade, to take up one of the twenty-minute watches observed at the foot of the catafalque on which the coffin rested. Queen Mary was so moved by her sons' gesture that she commissioned F.E. Beresford to commemorate the scene in a painting known as *The Vigil of the Princes*.

CHAPTER TEN
YEAR OF THE THREE KINGS

Since the death of Queen Mary's colourfully engaging, if maverick brother, 'Frank', Prince Francis of Teck, in 1910 royal wills have always been sealed and denied public scrutiny. On New Year's Day 1936, however, one bequest from a royal will was disclosed when it emerged that Princess Victoria had left Coppins, her estate in Iver, to her nephew, Prince George.

Between March and June that year, considerable alterations were made to the house before the Duke and Duchess of Kent adopted it as their country home. A curiously shaped porch was demolished together with a verandah that Princess Victoria had built so that she might enjoy the view of the lawns and the countryside beyond; most of the original fireplaces were taken out in favour of modern replacements, while George, the keenest motorist in the family, had the existing garage pulled down and a new one, featuring high-pressure hoses and air supply, built to his own specifications. Inside the house, once Princess Victoria's possessions had been removed, Prince George dispelled the Victorian gloom by again using delicate colour schemes, light pine panelling and bright fabrics. (One of the few objects belonging to Aunt Toria that the Kents did keep was a marble bust of Edward VII, which was allowed to remain in the entrance hall). To lighten the rooms still further, the duke tackled the garden's heavy vegetation and helped fell trees that restricted the flow of natural light.

While the builders and decorators were at work George and Marina paid frequent visits to the house and, on one particular Friday in April, they were accompanied by Queen Mary, the Duke and Duchess of York, Princess Alice and her husband Lord Athlone (Queen Mary's youngest brother 'Alge'), with whom they had been lunching at Royal Lodge, the Yorks' pink-stuccoed house in Windsor Great Park.

Of the rooms on the ground floor – which also included a dining room to seat fourteen, and two sitting rooms – the large music room with its tall glass doors opening on to the garden became the main salon. Here, George would listen to jazz records, play his Ibeck baby grand or the larger Steinway, or quietly sit and read while Marina painted at her easel, set up on a dustsheet spread over the carpet. Here also the Kents would entertain their friends. On any evening Noël Coward might be found at Coppins, as might other musicians, writers and actors such as Malcolm Sargent, Somerset Maugham, Douglas Fairbanks and an assortment of relations including George's cousin 'Dickie' Mountbatten and his wife Edwina. Other guests included the Channons, who first visited towards the end of 1936. In his diary for 1 November, Chips Channon wrote, 'We drove down to Coppins to call on the Kents. They have modernised and re-decorated [the house] with skill and success. The result is charming, and the rooms now glow with luxe and gaiety. It is entirely Prince George who has trans-formed it, and he now thinks of little else. We had a massive yea, and then the besotted father carried in ... the curly-haired, very red Prince Edward [who] looks like all four [Hanoverian] Georges rolled into one.'

There were also times that year when the king and Mrs Simpson drove over from Sunningdale either for tea or cocktails; and in return George and Marina were often entertained at the Fort. Whether it was because they were generally more open-minded and less conservative than the rest of the royal family, or were simply less willing to sit in judgement on others who didn't quite fit the tribal 'one of us' mould, Prince George and Princess Marina rather liked Wallis Simpson. It is true that their feel-ings cooled for a time after the Abdication to the extent that at one point George became so angry and distressed that he said he wanted to kill Mrs Simpson.

It is also true that in 1937 Marina flatly refused to visit the Duke and Duchess of Windsor, as David and Wallis had by then become, when she and George were on holiday in the Tyrol. Since nothing would move Marina, the duke made the trip to Castle Wasserleonburg in Carinthia on his own. When he arrived he was met by a tit-for-tat response, and

Marina's snub was repaid in kind, such that while George saw his brother, Wallis ensured he did not see her. But in time the hurts passed and the wounds healed and, as Princess Alexandra told the author, her parents never again lost touch with the Duke and Duchess of Windsor.

British history books record 1936 as the 'Year of the Three Kings'. On New Year's Day the reign of George V had only twenty days left to run. By 31 December the reign of his second son and namesake George VI was exactly twenty days old. In between had fallen the historic eleven-month reign of King Edward VIII.

Court mourning for George V meant that for the first few months of the year the Duke and Duchess of Kent were virtually free of public engagements. Privately they had more than enough to do and for the duke, as we have seen the refurbishment of Coppins was high on his list of priorities. For the duchess official inactivity meant she could fit in extra visits to her own family. Ever since their childhood Marina and her sisters had shared an affinity that was unusual in a family dominated by women. Throughout their lives, despite the inevitable responsibilities of adulthood, marriage and family life, they were ever in constant touch, exchanging long letters, long telephone calls and long visits. Not surprisingly, issues of motherhood had taken pride of place in the sisters' thoughts and conversations, from the time Princess Olga's sons Alexander and Nicholas were born. Now with Woolly the mother of Hans Viet, her first child born in January 1935, and Marina the devoted mother of Prince 'Eddie' as he was called, nine months younger than his German cousin, the three sisters had even more to talk about.

It was with children in mind that George and Marina set out for Belgrade at the beginning of April. For the past month Prince and Princess Paul had been settling into their newly-built home, an impressive neo-Palladian mansion approached through an avenue of lime trees, which Paul had named Beli Dvor or White Palace. It was there on 7 April that Olga gave birth to her third and youngest child, a longed-for daughter, whom they named Jelisavetta (Elisabeth), and to whom George and Marina were to act as godparents.

Though it was far too early for anyone to be certain at that stage, Marina was again pregnant; and confirmation of that fact led to a small family celebration when she and George paid yet another holiday visit to Belgrade in June. Two months later Prince Paul, both as regent and as a personal friend, received Marina's brother-in-law King Edward VIII when he paid a fleeting visit to Yugoslavia. The brevity of the King's stay that August suited Paul very well, since David had Mrs Simpson in tow and neither he nor Olga approved of the relationship that would soon cause a sensation throughout the world and cause a constitutional crisis at home in Britain. As a result of Prince Paul's attitude the atmosphere during the royal visit was at best strained. The Duchess of Windsor recalled in her memoirs, 'The meeting between the Balkan Prince and the British monarch was hardly calculated to hearten either Foreign Office. In a Slavic style worthy of his mountain-chieftain forebears, Paul led us in a wild motorcade through the countryside, scattering peasants and chickens in a flurry of blouses and feathers, curses and cackles. David had a number of comments on the excursion, the one that really amused me was 'This is just about what I expected. The only things that bothers me is that I can't figure which he cares less about, the peasants or the chickens or us.'

Edward VIII's courtesy call on the regent of Yugoslavia preceded the now famous cruise along the Dalmatian coast which he, Mrs Simpson, and a handful of friends including Lady Diana Cooper, took aboard Lady Yule's luxury steam yacht the *Nahlin*. Planned as a purely private holiday, the voyage soon assumed all the trappings of an official royal progress. Everywhere they stopped, from Yugoslavia to Turkey, kings, presidents and prime ministers turned out in force to welcome the British sovereign.

At home, the king's holiday was scarcely referred to by the press. Now and then a paragraph or two might appear, but even then no mention was made of David's companion. Not until 3 December, when the press could maintain its silence no longer, did the people of Britain and the empire learn what had been headline news and common gossip throughout Europe and America for the past two or three months: the king was in love with, and intended to marry, the by now twice-divorced Wallis Simpson.

Everywhere alarm bells started to ring. Queen Mary, who had understandably, if unfairly, branded Wallis an 'adventuress', was never more confirmed in her opinion that 'one divorce could seldom or never be justified, and to divorce twice, on any grounds whatsoever, was ... unthinkable.'

As heir presumptive, the Duke of York was brought to the point of nervous collapse at the thought of what he might have to take upon himself, while his wife, ever Mrs Simpson's most bitter opponent, joined the chorus of 'Establishment' figures determined to vilify Wallis as some kind of unspeakable sorceress, hell bent on luring Edward VIII to his doom, rather than seeing the situation for what it was and blaming the King for his inherent weakness of character and lack of dedication to his role as sovereign. Of the King's family, only the Duke of Kent wondered how David, as temporal governor of a Church that forbade divorce, could actually marry a divorcee *and* retain his crown. How, in one of the king's own favourite expressions, did David think he would be able 'to get away with it'? And what of Wallis? What would she become? What, as Prince George asked his brother, would 'she call herself?'

'Call herself?' the king replied. 'What do you think? "queen of England", of course!'

'She's going to be *queen*?' George asked in amazement.

'Yes,' cried the king, 'and empress of India – the whole bag of tricks.'

Not unnaturally the king wanted Wallis to share his throne as queen consort, but when it became obvious, even to him, that that could never be, the idea of a morganatic marriage, which had been suggested to Wallis over lunch at Claridge's by Esmond Harmsworth, chairman of the Newspaper Proprietors' Association, was proposed. It was not something that would work. The British government would not approve and nor would the governments of the dominions. The choice became ever clearer; either the king would have to renounce Mrs Simpson or the crown.

'I pointed out to him,' said his Prime Minister Stanley Baldwin, 'that the position of the King's wife was different from the position of any other citizen in the country; it was part of the price which the King had to pay. His wife becomes Queen; the Queen becomes Queen of the country; and therefore, in the choice of a Queen, the voice of the people must be heard.'

To Baldwin's utter astonishment the king then replied that as his marriage 'had become an indispensable condition to his continued existence' he had made up his mind ' ... I mean to abdicate to marry Mrs Simpson.'

Edward VIII's decision not only stunned the government and outraged his family, it also divided public opinion. On 25 November, Chips Channon confided to his diary, 'The possibility of a royal marriage is still the talk of London .... The Duke of Kent asked Kitty Brownlow [wife of the king's lord-in-waiting, Perry Brownlow] what she thought of 'this marriage'. Kitty tried to nance out, but he insisted. 'After all they are my relations.' Then he made an astonishing rejoinder: 'I am very discreet.' 'As discreet as a Chubb safe when you've given away all the keys,' Kitty retorted.'

Almost two weeks later, and only two days before the crisis reached its inexorable climax, Channon and his wife were at a dinner party given by Lady Cunard, when Chips was summoned to the telephone. Afterwards he wrote, 'I ... recognised the Duchess of Kent's voice. She asked us to go and see her, and Honor and I stole away to 3 Belgrave Square.... For two days now the Duke of Kent has been with his brother at the Fort, never leaving him for a second and trying by every means in his power to persuade him to stay. The King told him that over two years ago while he knew that he was an excellent Prince of Wales and liked his job, he nevertheless felt that he could never 'stick' being King as he puts it, he was afraid of being a bad one. He could never tolerate the restrictions, the etiquette, the loneliness; so perhaps if this issue had not arisen, something else would have.'

For weeks the peoples of the empire, from colonial top brass to the humblest of workers, had hung on to every word from London, denouncing or defending the king, depending on where their sympathies lay. In a prophetic letter written in early December to Lord Brabourne, governor of Bombay, 'Rab' Butler, who was then under-secretary of state at the India Office, said, 'I never give people my private views, but here they are. [the king] is a congenitally weak man with great personal charm, publicity sense, and some cunning.... He will abdicate and will be succeeded by a dull dog who will hold the declining influence of the Church and whose fortunes will be linked with that of the middle class.'

In less than a fortnight Butler's prophecy of abdication came to fruition. But before it did it appears there was a moment when the accession of the 'dull dog', as he called Bertie, Duke of York, was not a foregone conclusion, despite the fact that he was Edward VIII's rightful heir and next in line to the throne. In the weeks that led up first to Wallis Simpson's divorce in October, followed by the King's abdication six weeks later, certain high-placed voices questioned whether the ill-prepared, retiring Duke of York, plagued as he was by a stammer and given to sudden outbursts of temper, which his family called his 'gnashes', was the right man for the job. Indeed, he himself was panic-stricken by the thought of succeeding to the throne and the strain of it all brought him to the point of nervous collapse.

An alternative scenario involved the crown passing over the next four in line of succession - which is to say the Duke of York, his daughters Elizabeth, then aged ten, and Margaret, who was six, and his recently-married but as yet childless brother, Harry, Duke of Gloucester – to Prince George, Duke of Kent, who was not only married but already had a son and heir. According to one extremely well placed constitutional expert the idea was given serious consideration. In his book *Princess Elizabeth*, published with royal approval in 1947, Dermot Morrah, former Fellow of All Souls College, Oxford and Arundel Herald Extraordinary, who would write the famous speech Princess Elizabeth would broadcast on her twenty-first birthday, as well as several authorized royal books, told his readers that if Edward VIII 'must cease to be King, it would be necessary for Parliament to amend the Act of Settlement in order to give effect to his decision; and, as the constitutional lawyers who drafted the Bill did not fail to point out, if the Act of Settlement was to be changed it did not follow automatically that the next heir under that Act should succeed King Edward. The new Act must in effect name the new King; and in these unprecedented circumstances it was scarcely possible for Parliament to call any successor to the vacant throne without consulting his personal wishes ... It was certainly seriously considered at this time whether, by agreement among the Royal Family, the crown might not be settled on the Duke of Kent, the only one of the abdicating King's brothers who at that time had a son to become Prince of Wales, and so avoid laying so heavy a future burden upon the shoulders of any woman [namely Princess Elizabeth]. The possibility of such a course was debated by some men of authority in the State who believed that it would accord with the wishes of the royal persons concerned.'

Among the 'men of authority in the State' Dermot Morrah referred to was undoubtedly Sir Horace Wilson, a high-ranking civil servant who as special advisor to Prime Minister Stanley Baldwin played a key role in mediating between Downing Street and Buckingham Palace during the abdication crisis. In a report now housed in the National Archives that Sir Horace prepared was a note in an unattributed hand that was seen by the writer and journalist Christopher Wilson, which also lends weight to the idea that the Duke of Kent and not his elder brother was, for however long (we shall probably never know) considered as a possible king. The note an astonished Christopher Wilson saw read: 'Suggested that Queen Mary should be appointed Queen Regent until the divorce and the Abdication should be over.' The idea behind the suggestion was presumably to maintain the monarchy's stability at a moment of crisis under the control of the greatly respected queen dowager, while providing the parties most directly concerned with the time and space in which to decide which of the outgoing monarch's brothers should succeed him. In the event, as we well know, Edward VIII was rightfully succeeded by his brother the Duke of York.

On that fateful day, Thursday 10 December 1936, as the dukes of York, Gloucester and Kent made their way to the King's private retreat near Virginia Water, a dank, canopy-like fog hung over the Thames Valley as it had all week. That morning on Edward VIII's writing table in the octagonal drawing room at Fort Belvedere six copies of a document, embossed with the royal coat-of-arms and headed 'Instrument of Abdication', lay near a red leather despatch box on which the words 'The King' were embossed in gold block letters. When, at about 10am the royal dukes arrived they went immediately into the drawing room, where their elder brother awaited them. Moments later David sat down at the table and, for the last time in his brief but historic reign, signed each of the documents *Edward R.I.* 'It was all quite informal,' he would recall in his memoirs. 'When I had signed the last document I yielded the chair to my brothers, who in turn appended their signatures in their order of precedence.' Having discharged his last duty as king and emperor, David stepped outside, '... as if in harmony with the lifting of the almost intolerable pressure of the last few weeks', he wrote, 'the fog ... had also lifted.'

The following afternoon, while lunching at the Fort with Winston Churchill, Edward VIII ceased to reign. When it was time for the future Prime Minister to take leave of his old friend, David walked with him down the short stretch of hall to the front door. The former monarch was to recall, 'Something must have stirred in his mind. Tapping out the solemn measure with his walking stick, he began to recite, as if to himself: 'He nothing common did or mean, upon that memorable scene.' His resonant voice seemed to give an especial poignancy to these lines from the ode by Andrew Marvell, on the beheading of Charles I.'

By morning David would be sailing towards Boulogne-sur-Mer in northern France at the start of an exile that would end only with his death thirty-six years later, in May 1972. But before his midnight departure for Portsmouth, where he boarded the F-class destroyer HMS *Fury*, there was his farewell speech to the nation, which he broadcast from the Oak Room above the Sovereign's Entrance at Windsor Castle. More painfully, there were also his private farewells to his family. In the salon at Royal Lodge, Bertie and Elizabeth's retreat over in the Great Park, where they had assembled after dinner to hear David's broadcast, were Queen Mary, her younger sons Harry and George, her daughter Mary, the Princess Royal, her brother 'Alge', Lord Athlone, and his wife Princess Alice. When he returned from the castle, David – or 'His Royal Highness Prince Edward', as Sir John Reith, director-general of the BBC, had announced him – kissed his mother and each of his relations in turn. Then, bowing to Bertie, who had now become King George VI, he said, 'God bless you, Sir! I hope you will be happier than your predecessor.'

That scene, so heavily charged with pathos, proved too much for the sobbing Duke of Kent who in his anguish suddenly cried out, 'It isn't possible! It isn't happening!' Given the strength and depth of the bond he and David, who at the suggestion of the new king had now become HRH The Duke of Windsor, had long shared, George's distress and sense of personal loss at his brother's departure was, in all probability, far keener than that of any other member of his family. To others, such as the new king, his wife and mother, such sorrow as they may have felt was outweighed by anger and incomprehension at what they considered to be David's dereliction of duty.

In her unpublished memoirs Lady Iris Mountbatten, the only child of 'Drino', Marquess of Carisbrooke, a grandson of Queen Victoria, recalled that Queen Mary 'actually seemed unchanged by the great loss of her eldest son. I could see no outward sign that she had been tormented by heartbreak.... It brought home to me a sense that I had always had, that my family was not motivated by love or human emotions.'

Whatever the feelings of David's relations that December, the otherwise familiar routine of royal life went on and, as Christmas approached, most members of the royal family gathered as they always did at Sandringham. Two notable absentees, however, were the Duke and Duchess of Kent. With the birth of their second child due at any time, they had decided to remain at 3 Belgrave Square, with Prince and Princess Nicholas as their guests. There on Christmas morning, to the sound of a lone street musician playing carols on a penny whistle somewhere nearby, Princess Marina presented her husband with a daughter – Alexandra Helen Elizabeth Olga Christabel. The official announcement issued that afternoon told the country 'H.R.H. The Duchess of Kent was safely delivered of a daughter at 11.20 this morning. Her Royal Highness and the infant Princess are doing excellently.'

Celebrating the royal birth in traditional style, a battery of Royal Horse Artillery set up its guns in Hyde Park, at noon on Boxing Day, to fire a salute. This forty-one gun tribute was echoed by another fired simultaneously from the Tower of London. Five days later still in celebratory mood, the baby's father seized New Year's Eve as an opportunity to dress up in a silver Tyrolean costume to accompany Lady Caroline Paget and the Honourable David Herbert to the Chelsea Arts Ball.

In Austria, where Prince George's outfit might have looked more at home, the Duke of Windsor had spent Christmas Day as the guest of Britain's ambassador Sir Walford Selby and his wife. A few days later, he greeted the New Year in quaint fashion at Schloss Enzefeld, near Vienna, which had been his base since he arrived from France on 14 December. On the stroke of midnight David was given a sucking pig to hold which, according to custom, would bring good luck in the year ahead.

CHAPTER ELEVEN
THE DUKE AND THE GELLIBRAND

Scarcely had the New Year begun than the Duke of Kent found himself at the centre of what the press, with its ear for a good royal story, turned into a minor scandal; the inference being that Prince George was again playing away from home. The episode had started in apparent innocence on 1 January. That morning, beneath headline news that Mussolini was to ban Italian volunteers from joining the Spanish Civil War, and sandwiched between a goodwill message from George VI, the engagement of tennis star Betty Nuthall, and news of the Third Test in Melbourne, the *Daily Express* ran an entertaining article about the visit of the duke and a certain 'Mrs Allen' to Miss Evelyn Bool at the London Phrenological Institution at Ludgate Circus, Fleet Street. There the pair had their heads 'read' by the elderly Miss Bool who, by feeling the contours of a person's head, claimed to be able to reveal their abilities, characteristics and pursuits in which they were most likely to succeed.

Miss Bool, who was reported to have been 'thrilled by her fifteen-minute reading of a royal head', said afterwards, that the Duke of Kent had 'A very nicely balanced head. I should say a fine quality of brain matter rather than quantity. If he were out in the world looking for a job, he would be best suited for classical or artistic work.' In itself it was all harmless stuff and as such it might have remained had not the *Express* asked on its front page next day, 'Who is Mrs Allen?' Under a photograph of a dark, sultry beauty, the paper's gossip columnist 'William Hickey' provided the answer by telling its readers that she was 'Mrs William Allen, wife of a wealthy business man who was formerly M.P. for West Belfast and is an authority on the peoples of the Near East.

'As Miss Paula Gellibrand – 'The Gellibrand' – she was London's most beautiful mannequin in 1922, and was painted by many artists. As the Marquise de Casa Maury [predecessor of Freda Dudley-Ward, who in October 1937, married the marquis, after divorcing her first husband] she became one of the best-known figures in the social circle in which the Duke and Duchess of Kent move.'

From then on, rumours that Prince George and Mrs Allen, who had been one of Cecil Beaton's favourite and often photographed models, were having an affair became widespread. But on 16 January, the *Evening Standard's* gossip column 'Londoner's Diary' – ostensibly in an attempt to put a stop to the stories – declared that the consequences of the couple's visit to Miss Evelyn Bool had been '... ludicrous and – to members of the royal family and Mrs Allen – extremely painful. His Royal Highness has been the recipient of a flood of letters, most of them anonymous, describing the occasion in terms varying from crude innuendo to open accusation.

'Rumour's latest guise is that, in consequence of the Duke's relationship with Mrs Allen, divorce proceedings have already been instituted by her husband [married in 1932 they did, in fact, divorce in 1939].

'For the past three years,' the article went on, 'Mr and Mrs 'Bill' Allen have been living almost entirely in Ireland. On one of their rare visits to London Mrs Allen, who has been a friend of the Duke's since his midshipman days, called at Belgrave Square ... to see the Duchess and her newly-born daughter.'

It wasn't long before the press tired of its own intrigue, though not before Eton-educated 'Bill' Allen had spoken up for himself in the columns of *The Times* and in so doing issued a thinly veiled threat to the perpetrators of the scandal by saying '... certain individuals, who have grown rich upon the ruthless exploitation of other people's lives, will find that they have come into conflict with men who are not in such a helpless position as some who have recently been tortured on the wheel of the yellow Press.'

As the episode slipped from mind, so it was replaced by escalating public and media interest in the forthcoming coronation of King George VI and Queen Elizabeth on Wednesday 12 May 1937. That date had originally been set for the coronation of Edward VIII and as many of the arrangements were already well advanced before his abdication pressed the pause button, it was decided to leave things as they were. After all, nothing save the man who was now about to be crowned, had changed.

On coronation morning as the new king and queen and their two daughters Elizabeth and Margaret prepared themselves at nearby Buckingham Palace for the long day ahead, George and Marina were also woken early. The duke, who was to ride as part of the escort behind the immense gold state coach that had been built for George III in 1762, in which George VI and Queen Elizabeth would travel to and from Westminster Abbey, where over thirty coronations had taken place in its long history, was helped into his ceremonial naval uniform. Next door Marina who, in the words of Edward Molyneux ranked 'with the Empress Eugénie among the world's outstanding leaders of fashion', put on a slender gown of gold tissue, embroidered with frond-like sequinned feathers. George, as the king's brother, would take part in the coronation ritual by swearing fealty to his sovereign, while Marina, sitting between the Duchess of Gloucester and the Countess of Strathmore (the queen's mother) watched the proceedings from the royal gallery near the high altar.

Just three weeks later on the other side of the Channel, another smaller and altogether more private royal ceremony took place. At the Château de Candé near Tours in the Loire Valley, on Thursday 3 June, the Duke of Windsor and Wallis Simpson were married.

'Almost every newspaper ... has run a leader of good wishes ...' Chips Channon noted in his diary. 'The Times, however, refrained. It is of course an organ of the Archbishop [of Canterbury, the meddlesome Dr Cosmo Gordon Lang] and he is a power behind it. I think it is disgraceful. The treatment of the Duke of Windsor by the present Government has hurt the institution of royalty far more than ever the Duke of Windsor did himself by his abdication.'

Younger members of the royal family felt much the same way. Echoing the views of Lady Iris Mountbatten, the late Earl of Harewood, elder son of Mary, Princess Royal, recalled in his memoirs, '... it was hard for the younger among us not to stand in amazement at the moral contradiction between the elevation of code of duty on the one hand, and on the other the denial of central Christian virtues – forgiveness, understanding, family tenderness.'

For some time David had hoped that his brother George would be able to travel to France to act as his best man. In reality it was a vain and naïve hope. As the Home Secretary, Sir John Simon, advised the king, if any member of the royal family were to attend the wedding, it would 'be regarded, and represented, as accepting the future Duchess *for all purposes* into the Royal circle ... [and] If, for example, it is desired to *dis*courage [the duke and duchess's] return to this country, absence from the wedding could be indicative of a desire to maintain a certain aloofness.'

George, like Harry Gloucester, did send David and Wallis a wedding present, while Queen Mary, together with Bertie and Elizabeth, telegraphed their best wishes. Otherwise there was nothing – well, not quite nothing. On the eve of his wedding, the incredulous bridegroom received a letter from the king advising him that Wallis would not be granted the style and rank of Royal Highness. What that meant, in effect, was that George VI and his ministers were giving David as Duke of Windsor something he had suggested and been denied as king – a morganatic marriage.

Though no members of the royal family attended David's wedding, there was hardly one of them who did not want to hear every detail from 'Baba' Metcalfe, who had been one of the fifteen or so personal guests at the Château de Candé, and whose husband 'Fruity' had acted as the Duke of Windsor's best man in place of Prince George. 'The King and Queen, Prince George and Princess Marina wanted to know everything,' she said. 'But after I told them, the subject was never mentioned again.'

Another invitee that June, though not as a guest on the day itself, was Cecil Beaton, who had been asked to photograph David and Wallis in their wedding finery; the former king in his morning suit and the former Mrs Simpson, she had reverted to her maiden name Warfield by deed poll less than a month before, in her soft blue crêpe de soie dress and jacket designed by the Paris-based, American couturier who, by combining his first and last names (Main and Bocher) became famous as Mainbocher. But while the Duke and Duchess of Windsor like the Duchess of Gloucester were among his many sitters, Beaton yearned to photograph the Duchess of Kent (Wallis's only equal when it came to chic and style), in whom he admired 'the cool classical features in a perfect oval head held high on a straight column of neck, the topaz eyes, the slightly tilted smile, the apricot complexion, and the nut-brown camp of flat silken curls.' Marina had already sat for several other celebrated photographers, notably Dorothy Wilding, Horst, Harlip and Bassano, and she had been painted by Philip de Laszlo and Saveley Sorine. But Beaton had yet to receive a summons. When it finally came during the summer of 1937 he was jubilant. Of their first sitting, he wrote breathlessly, 'The Duchess looked excessively beautiful in a huge brown tulle crinoline, ruched like a Queen Anne window blind, or a lampshade, with old-fashioned jewellery. She looked like a Winterhalter painting and it was thus that she was photographed, slightly nervous at first and very Royal, with her deep, clipped accented voice, but soon she was as pliable as any sitter I have ever had and we made many jokes and got along splendidly.' It was the start of a warm and life-long friendship during which Beaton would photograph Marina – and her family – on numerous occasions. Later in life, he would recall 'the many photographic sessions in the garden at Coppins with her husband and children, and, at the studio, when she would arrive with a picnic lunch-basket and boxes containing Greek national dress and her formal gown complete with orders and decorations.'

In July the Duke and Duchess of Kent were preparing for their summer holiday. For Marina a few days with Eddie and seven-month-old Alexandra, at Bloody Point, a converted coast-guard station at Shingle End near Sandwich in Kent, would precede a visit by car to Germany. There she and George would stay with Toto and Woolly – whose second child Helen Marina Elisabeth, had been born that May – before going on to friends in Lancut, Poland, and ending up as usual with Olga and Paul at their home in Yugoslavia.

On 27 July, Marina, casual but elegant in a polka-dot dress, light blouson jacket, two-tone shoes and gloves, left Belgrave Square with her children for Shingle End. *En route* her car was involved in a serious collision with another. Miraculously no one was injured. Though badly shaken, Marina gathered up a rug and spread it out in a field where she helped comfort the family. The holder of a nearby coffee stall had rushed to their assistance and, at the duchess's request, had telephoned for a relief car to collect them.

Four months later, in a profoundly tragic event that foreshadowed one that was to occur in not dissimilar circumstances in 1942, the royal family was devastated by the loss in an air crash of Marina's first cousin – and the future Duke of Edinburgh's sister – Cecilie, Hereditary Grand Duchess of Hesse and by Rhine, her husband, the Hereditary Grand Duke Georg Donatus ('Don' as he was known), their two young sons, Ludwig and Alexander, Don's mother, the widowed Grand Duchess Eleonore, the children's nurse, a family friend and the two-man aircrew. Making the loss of the family even more unbearable was the discovery of the tiny body of a new born son lying next to his mother, Cecilie.

The tragedy happened while the grand ducal family was *en route* to London for the marriage of Don's younger brother Prince Louis and Margaret Geddes, the only daughter of Sir Auckland Geddes, a former British ambassador to the United States and his wife Isabella. Four days ahead of the wedding which was to have taken place at St Peter's, Eaton Square, on 20 November, in the presence of most of the royal family, the grand ducal party left Frankfurt to fly to Croydon Aerodrome aboard a three-engined Junkers Ju52 aircraft of Sabena Airways. At Steene, near Ostend, one hour after take-off, the aircraft encountered a sudden dense fog that had drifted in from the sea. Despite the fact that visibility was down to just twenty feet, it is believed – and the subsequent Belgian inquiry into the crash suggested – that the pilot was attempting to land at Ostend because the heavily-pregnant hereditary grand duchess had gone into labour. But as the plane descended, it clipped the top of a brickworks chimney and as one of the wings and one of the engines, were ripped off the aircraft plummeted in flames into the brickworks below. There were no survivors.

The wedding of Louis and Margaret, which had already been post-poned by the death in October of the prince's father, Grand Duke Ernst Ludwig IV, brother of the last Russian tsarina Alexandra and of Ella, Grand Duchess Elisabeth Feodorovna, was brought forward by three days and in an air of funereal gloom took place quietly at St Peter's, early on the morning of 17 November.

The following February George and Marina were holidaying at St Anton with Woolly and Toto, when they received word from Athens that Prince Nicholas, who had returned to Greece three months earlier and who had become unwell soon afterwards, was dying of arteriosclerosis. Perhaps because Marina disliked flying she, Woolly and their husbands caught the night train from Munich. Time lost as a result of the longer rail journey meant that two of the prince's three daughters were not with him when he died at the Hotel Grand Bretagne, on 8 February. When *en route*, the train stopped in Belgrade, Prince Paul was there to meet it. It was he who had the sorry task of telling Marina and Elizabeth that, during the night, their father's condition had grown worse and that shortly after a priest had administered Extreme Unction, Prince Nicholas whispered to his wife and eldest daughter, 'I am happy to die in my own beloved country,' and had then slipped into a coma.

Prince Nicholas was remembered by Chips Channon as 'A gentle, dreamy gentleman ... particularly devoted to the late George V, who was his first cousin. To him, he was in the habit of sending naughty stories and doubtful limericks; for the late King had a racy mind and liked a vulgar joke, so long as the point was obvious.'

Upon their arrival in Athens, the Duchess of Kent and Countess Toerring went straight to their parents' suite at the Grand Bretagne and, with their mother and sister, sat by their father's body for fifteen minutes. Four days later, following a lying in state in the Metropolitan Cathedral, during which thousands queued to pay their respects, the 65-year-old prince was given a state funeral before his remains were borne on a flag-draped, horse-drawn gun carriage to Tatoi, where he was buried near the graves of his parents. For the first five or six months of her widowhood, Princess Nicholas was taken care of by Princess Olga. Eventually, having decided to settle permanently in Athens, the princess found a comfortable suburban villa and there, becoming increasingly eccentric and surrounded by a number of pet cats, she remained until her own death almost twenty years later.

In the three years since her marriage the Duchess of Kent as a working member of the royal family had accepted two presidencies: the YWCA Central Club for Women and Girls, and Alexandra Rose Day, the fundraising charity which her great-aunt Queen Alexandra had established in 1912. She had also become patron of the Central School of Speech and Drama and the Elizabeth Garrett Anderson Hospital. Over the next quarter of a century as patron or president she would become actively involved with a further sixty-six diverse organizations that included the PDSA (People's Dispensary for Sick Animals), the Royal National Lifeboat Institution, the Anglo-Hellenic League, the Old Vic Theatre, Queen Victoria Seamen's Rest (The Seamen's Mission of the Methodist Church), the Army Winter Sports Association, the War Widows' Guild of Australia, the Royal Alexandra and Albert School, and the All England Lawn Tennis Club at Wimbledon.

For his part the Duke of Kent was no less popular among the communities he served in an official capacity, trying, as he put it, 'to gain a real appreciation of this country's problems by personal contact.' It was in recognition of his brother's achievements – and, no doubt, in tribute to the days when they were called 'The Foreman' and 'The Factory Inspector' – that George VI invited the duke to become the eleventh Governor-General of Australia, in succession to the 1st Earl of Gowrie who had held the post for a record nine years.

George's appointment was to take effect from November 1939 and, to that end, he set about making enthusiastic plans: relinquishing the lease on 3 Belgrave Square; arranging to ship some of his and Marina's furniture out to Government House in Canberra; and again selecting colour schemes, furnishing fabrics, and so on with which to 'revolutionize' the look of their new and even more impressive home. In her biography of Princess Marina, Stella King wrote, 'Curtains, hangings and tailored covers without traditional flounces were sent from England. [The duke] chose oatmeal-coloured silk tweed curtains, pale blue satin-covered sofas and chairs, and white Grecian rugs, which pleased the Duchess. The Duke also ordered £5,000 worth of household linen, which he paid for himself and included peach-coloured silk sheets edged with satin at £50 a pair.'

The Australians themselves seemed delighted by the Duke of Kent's appointment. 'It is the greatest compliment the Throne can pay to the Australian people,' said the *Sydney Sun,* while at home, Winston Churchill considered it a 'master-stroke of Imperial policy'. Only Marina winced at the prospect of living on the other side of the world, so very far away from her family, in a country that was not then noted for its gentility or culture. Indeed, if Australians were as eager to know her as contemporary reports suggest, Marina was hard put to return the compliment.

In the event, world affairs put an end to the Kents' plans. On 3 September, only two months before they were due to leave England, the duchess was listening to the wireless in the music room at Coppins, when it was announced that Britain was again at war with Germany.

CHAPTER TWELVE
DEAR MR PRESIDENT

During the early months of the Second World War George, Duke of Kent, found himself in naval uniform once more. This time, however, it was not the ceremonial kind tinkling with stars, orders and token medals, but the sober rig of an officer reporting for desk duty at the Admiralty. All too soon, however, he decided it was an 'awful waste of time' and for the second time in his life wanted out of Britain's senior service. What he wanted, he told his brother-in-law, Paul of Yugoslavia, was something that 'would be really useful to the country.' Telling Paul that he had petitioned the Prime Minister, he went on, '... we are used for anything and everything in peace, but when war comes no-one wants us.'

Although the king had not long 'promoted' George to Rear Admiral, he agreed to his transfer to the Royal Air Force with the rank of Air Vice-Marshal. To some extent, the Duke of Kent's duties in the RAF reflected the kind of work he had undertaken for the Home Office Factory Inspectorate, though the focus had now shifted from overseeing safety regulations and working conditions to boosting workers' morale. In the performance of these duties, George dropped the rank conferred on him by the king, in favour of that of Group Captain. The reason for this was to avoid him being placed, no matter how nominally, in a superior position to the senior officers under whom he would have to work.

By this time, Marina also found herself in uniform as Commandant of the Women's Royal Naval Service – otherwise known as the Wrens. Smart though the navy blue skirt and jacket, white shirt and dark tie were, the duchess was not enamoured of having to wear it. Indeed, she would not have done had Churchill himself not made it clear that she was required to do so. That aside, Marina was, as Jennifer Ellis wrote, 'the most conscientious of commandants, and the post was anything but a nominal one. She travelled all over the country, visiting all the chief centres of the WRNS, never sparing herself a tiring or difficult journey. She brought a human touch to even a routine inspection. Walking down a line of girls, she would stop to talk to each one personally, not just a conventional sentence or two, but with genuine interest.'

What might be called the 'Marina effect' did more for the image, recruitment and morale of the Wrens than any costly poster campaign would have achieved. 'Every time her photo appeared in the press in her uniform,' Dame Vera Laughton Matthews, Director of the WRNS, recalled 'there was a rush to join up.' And much as she may not have liked wearing it, the Duchess of Kent had a hand in the design of the uniform; which is to say that she, together with the director and the First Lord of the Admiralty put their heads together over a change in the style of hat to be worn by the Wrens. 'It's very important to recruiting' Marina said. 'No woman wants to wear a hat that makes her look unattractive, war or no war.'

From the time of her appointment right through to the eventual cessation of hostilities five years later, Marina's personal touch proved inspirational. Dame Vera said of her, 'Wherever she went on her tours of inspection she gave enormous pleasure. She insisted on seeing the girls' quarters and on finding out whether they were comfortable. She visited the galleys [which she insisted on calling 'kitchens'] and talked to the cooks. Young people are always quick to recognize sincerity. The girls felt that the duchess took a personal interest in them, and that she really cared whether they were happy or not.'

It was in that spirit of personal involvement that the Duchess of Kent agreed to appeal for yet more recruits. Her broadcast which was seen on film as well as broadcast on the wireless on 20 January 1941 brought, in the words of the Director, 'an immediate response from all over the country.' In part, Marina said 'Since February 1940, when I became Commandant of the Women's Royal Naval Service, I have been able to visit a number of ports where units of the Wrens are employed. I had always heard what a wonderful spirit of friendship existed throughout the organization. As a result of my visits, I know this was no exaggeration and I also know why.

Wren officers are promoted from the ranks and so they understand the conditions of life and work among the ratings with whom they have to deal....'

During her broadcast, Marina highlighted the importance of roles across the entire spectrum of service life, cooks and stewards, clerks and book-keepers, wireless telegraphists, switchboard operators, shorthand typists, and so on. All were needed. 'It may mean a sacrifice to leave your home and possibly work that interests you,' Marina concluded, 'but you will have the feeling that your new work is essential to our war effort. In this connection, I should like to say a word of congratulations to the many thousands of Wrens who are already serving their country. We are very proud of the wonderful way in which you have carried on your work during air raids and at times of tension. We admire your courage and we know that danger is met unflinchingly, because the future happiness of our families and homes depends on victory. If you join the Wrens, you will know that you have done your share and are worthy of your country.'

The Royal Navy was not the Duchess of Kent's only wartime involvement. At the very start she offered her services to the Iver and Denham Cottage Hospital, which had opened a few years earlier, and there, along with several other local volunteers, she made dressings, splints, swabs and helped generally. Later she went to work at University College Hospital in central London as a nursing auxiliary.

At the time, a Miss Bond was the nursing sister of Ward 16. She recalled, '... the matron sent for me one day and told me that the Duchess of Kent was to work on my ward .... She was to be known as Nurse Kay and her identity was to be a close secret. The Registrar and Senior Surgeon obviously knew what was afoot but the news didn't leak out for the first few weeks.' That it did leak out sooner than anybody might have wished was due to one vigilant patient, a dressmaker's assistant, who kept a close watch on the fashion columns. Having been told repeatedly that the royal lookalike was only 'Nurse Kay', the patient in question finally declared triumphantly, 'That VAD [Voluntary Aid Detachment] *is* the Duchess of Kent. I've seen her pictures dozens of times. Nobody is going to tell me it isn't her.'

During her 'anonymous' period at the hospital, of which she became patron in 1942, Princess Marina '... came and went as much as she liked – or as official commitments would permit. She took part in all routine activities in the ward – surgical dressings, bed making, washing patients, doing hair, tidying lockers, plumping up pillows, feeding and handing round meals on trays. She assisted in the pre-operational preparation of patients who were due for the theatre ... and the removal of tubes after the operations was also part of her job.'

As with other members of the royal family, news of the wartime engagements of both the Duke and the Duchess of Kent was carefully censored. Visits to factories, air raid precaution depots, hospitals, rest centres, fire stations and the like were never announced in advance and press items that appeared afterwards only provided the briefest of details. According to James Wentworth-Day, the duke '... went down to the East End dozens of times whilst air raids were on and was in one shelter, holding no less than 7,000 people whilst the place shuddered to bomb-blast. One time a bomb blew up with a terrific explosion within yards of his car. Bricks, broken glass and debris rained down. The Duke stopped his car, got out, perfectly unperturbed, walked across to a group of people, and said, 'That was a near thing, wasn't it? I am very glad to see that none of you are hurt.'

One delicate diplomatic mission that was entrusted to Prince George at this time called for all the charm, warmth and diplomacy at his command. In June 1940 Winston Churchill selected him to fly to Portugal to call upon the Prime Minister, Dr Antonio Salazar. Though ostensibly heading the British delegation attending the 800th anniversary celebrations of Portuguese independence, the real purpose of the duke's task was twofold. First it was to reaffirm the historic friendship that had existed between Britain and Portugal since the fourteenth-century, and second, to reassure the strictly neutral Salazar that Britain's position in the war was not the lost cause German propaganda would have him believe. Returning to London on 2 July, the duke – and by definition the British government - was secure in the knowledge that the sympathies of the Portuguese dictator were with Britain and her allies.

The following year, from late July to early September, George, who had recently been promoted to the rank of Air Commodore, and who was eager for further purposeful assignments, was scheduled to undertake a goodwill visit to Canada in order to inspect air training schools. At his suggestion he also went on to visit his friends the Roosevelts in the United States. It would not only be an important diplomatic gesture – a personal 'thank you' from the king's brother for American aid – but it would also provide him with a chance to see something of American factories engaged in the war effort. Moreover, George, who was still at heart dissatisfied with the work he was doing, hoped it might lead to a more substantial opportunity to utilize his 'ambassadorial' abilities.

Approved in London, the duke's proposal was put forward to Lord Halifax, Britain's ambassador in Washington. From his office on 24 July 1941 a letter was sent to the President informing him of the purpose of the Duke of Kent's tour of Canada, and adding that 'His Royal Highness ... would very much like to take the opportunity of paying a visit of courtesy to you .... It has also been suggested that the Duke while in the United States might visit one of the dockyards engaged in repairing a British warship, and possibly a factory producing aircraft for Great Britain.'

On 2 August, President Roosevelt approved the schedule for the Duke of Kent's three-day visit, which was arranged to take place from 23 to 26 August. Three weeks later George flew into New York's La Guardia airport and for the first thirty-six hours of his visit relaxed with Franklin and Eleanor Roosevelt at Hyde Park, their family home in New York State, before accompanying the president to Washington and the start of more formal activities.

On Monday 25 August, Prince George flew to Norfolk in Virginia, to visit the National Advisory Committee for Aeronautics laboratory. The following day it was on to Baltimore where he inspected the Glenn Martin aircraft factory, addressed the 10,000-strong workforce, and remained to lunch. Back in Washington early that evening, George toured the Capitol, the Supreme Court, the Washington Monument and the Lincoln Memorial, before visiting the Mellon Art Gallery, attending a cocktail party given by the National Press Club, and meeting Dominion ministers at the British Embassy. After the duke's visit Eleanor Roosevelt said, 'I think what impresses me most of all in meeting English people today is the great strain under which they have been and their sense of obligation in fulfilling whatever they consider is their duty. In coming to Canada and the United States, they represent the British people and they try in every way to express to us the appreciation they feel for the constant flow of aid from this country.'

In a cable to the Roosevelts which he sent from Hamilton, Ontario the day after he returned to Canada, the Duke of Kent reinforced those sentiments when he said, 'On leaving your country I would like to thank you, Mr President and Mrs Roosevelt, once again for your wonderful kindness and hospitality during my stay. I am deeply appreciative of the opportunity which was given to me to see something of what your country is doing to help Britain and I am greatly impressed with what is being done and what can be done.'

From The Citadel on Cap Diamant in Quebec, official residence of both the Sovereign and the Governor-General, Prince George reiterated his thanks in more personal letters to both Franklin and Eleanor Roosevelt. Addressing himself to the president, the duke, in his distinctive hand, wrote, 'I waited until my arrival here before writing to thank you once more for all your kindness ... during my visit to [the] USA. I cannot thank you enough for having me stop with you & for giving me the opportunity of talking to you & hearing your views on so many subjects. The gratitude of the British people for what you have done for us is immeasurable - & their admiration is unbounded – but I feel I must add my own word of admiration for all you are doing.... I was so glad to see something of your forces & also of the naval & air force plants. The Glenn Martin factory is most impressive – I am only sorry my stay was so short & that I was unable to see more.

'I have had a very rushed trip since I left Washington & only arrived here yesterday to stay with the Athlones [his aunt and uncle, Princess Alice, Countess of Athlone and the Earl of Athlone, who was Governor-General of Canada from 1940 to 1946]. I leave for England some time next week & shall take back to the King not only many messages from you but also many heartening words of all I have seen in your country.'

Between their official duties George and Marina tried to preserve some sense of normality in what, during the war years, passed for home life. As parents, both the Duke and the Duchess of Kent were devoted to Eddie and Alexandra; scuttling home in time for the children's tea on days when they had public engagements to perform, playing games, telling bedtime stories, showing them off to friends, and savouring the small incidents and childish sayings treasured by most parents. At the age of five or six, Eddie had already started to show signs of his father's love of cars and all things mechanical, and at Coppins father and son would spend hours tinkering about in the garage. To the young prince, the duke was also the fount of all knowledge, and there is a story that when he was in hospital having his tonsils out, Eddie asked his mother, 'How many bricks are there in the hospital, mummy?' Marina confessed she hadn't a clue nor, when asked, had the matron, of course. A little later, the boy proudly proclaimed that his father had solved the mystery. Greatly impressed, but nevertheless curious, the matron took the duke aside and asked him how he had found the answer. 'I didn't,' he replied, 'but for heaven's sake don't tell my son that I'm a liar.'

Like most children, Prince Edward and his sister were boisterous and at times clumsy, as happened at the end of one of Chips Channon's visits to the family. '... afternoon tea ended in tragedy,' he noted in his diary, 'as Little Edward became bumptious and knocked over a table, spilling a kettle of hot water over his little pink legs .... The Duke lost his temper, the Duchess was in a flurry, nannies rushed in, but little Alexandra, delightfully unconcerned, turned round, and as if to change the subject said, 'I love soldiers, do you?'

The Kents' third child and second son was born at Coppins at 7.35pm on Saturday 4 July 1942. For once the Home Secretary – who was traditionally present at a royal birth, or at least in the next room – was absent. The then incumbent, Herbert Morrison, was too tied up with extra duties as Minister of Home Security to waste valuable time playing lip service to a custom originally established in 1688. At that distant time, when the wars of religion were still fresh in people's minds, the unfounded rumour was spread that James II's wife Mary of Modena had been delivered of a stillborn child and a Catholic 'changeling' had subsequently been slipped into the royal bed in a warming pan. As a result, the king had introduced the requirement for an independent witness to be present at future royal births. Anachronistic though it had long since become – and the tradition was not finally abolished until 1948 when Princess Elizabeth was expecting the birth of Prince Charles – the Home Secretary had no choice but to accept the Duke of Kent's word that the latest addition to the royal family was indeed legitimate.

With the birth of their youngest child having come on a day of such national importance in the United States, George and Marina decided to ask Franklin Roosevelt to become one of the infant's godparents. Two days later, in the way of diplomatic niceties, their invitation was formally extended to the president via John Winant, then American ambassador to the Court of St James's. Cabling Washington, he said, 'The Duke of Kent has just sent me the following note. "My wife and I would be so delighted if you would be godfather to our son. We should be especially pleased, as he was born on Independence Day". On 11 July Roosevelt responded, 'I am much thrilled and very proud to be Godfather to the youngster and I send him my affectionate greetings. Tell the Duchess that I count on seeing him as soon as the going is good.'

This rather curious form of communication between friends continued just over a fortnight later on 28 July, when Ambassador Winant sent a further telegram to the president, marked 'Triple Priority'. It read, 'The Duke of Kent has asked me to send you the following message: "We are so pleased you are to be Godfather. Christening takes place August 4th at Windsor Castle. The King will stand proxy for you". On the day of the service itself the president cabled the duke, 'My affectionate regards to Michael George Charles Franklin. I am anxious to see him as soon as I can. Do send me his photograph. Tell the King that I will hold him to strict accountability until I am able to take over the responsibility of a godfather myself. My warm regards to you and the Duchess. Franklin D. Roosevelt.'

Until the end of the war, which in 1942 still lay three years distant, family happiness for Marina, her sisters, and their sixty-year-old mother was clouded by their enforced separation. Woolly and her Bavarian husband Count Toerring were officially Britain's enemies; Princess Nicholas lived under German occupation in her suburban villa outside Athens; while Olga and Paul were under house arrest in Kenya for alleged treason.

This is not the place for a lengthy discussion of Yugoslav politics but, briefly, Prince Paul's fall came about in March 1941 when, by yielding to ever-increasing pressure from Germany and her allies, he was forced into signing a Tripartite Pact which, in essence, guaranteed Yugoslavia freedom from attack as long as German troops and equipment were allowed free passage through to Greece. Despite an overwhelming vote in favour of this move from within the Yugoslav cabinet itself, Prince Paul – a regent with 'too many neighbours and too few friends', as he was later described – was branded a traitor and quisling. Exile followed, and in April 1941 Prince and Princess Paul, now regarded as political prisoners, were *en route* to Kenya. There, under British jurisdiction, they were to be held at a Moroccan-style house called Osserian, on the shores of Lake Naivasha, which had been the home of Josslyn Hay, Earl of Erroll, of Happy Valley fame, whose unsolved murder in 1941 caused a sensation.

Accusations of treason and subsequent house arrest for Prince Paul was a harsh penalty for a man whose sympathies had always been fiercely pro-British and who, as regent, had attempted to steer a course that was in line with the country he so profoundly admired. But for the Duchess of Kent the defamatory speeches in the House of Commons, and the attacks upon her sister and brother-in-law that were published in the British press, were no less difficult to bear.

Throughout the war, communication with her mother and sisters was difficult though not impossible. Even so, there were times when Marina felt acutely alone without the kind of intimate companionship she, Olga and Elizabeth had shared for more than thirty years. But for the moment at least, the duchess had her husband in whom to find comfort and support.

CHAPTER THIRTEEN
A TRAGIC MYSTERY

Between 25 August 1941, when he visited the NACA laboratory in Norfolk, Virginia, and his death exactly one year later, the Duke of Kent had flown more than 60,000 miles on active service with the Royal Air Force. Another 1,800 miles would have been added to his record, had his scheduled mission to inspect RAF bases in Iceland been accomplished according to plan.

For the duke and duchess much of August had been taken up, one way and another, with family events. On the fourth, their one-month-old son Michael was christened in the private chapel at Windsor Castle, where, aside from President Roosevelt, his seven other godparents (King George VI; Queen Wilhelmina of the Netherlands; King Haakon VII of Norway; Frederica, Hereditary Princess of Greece; Victoria, Dowager Marchioness of Milford Haven and Lady Patricia Ramsay) were either present in person or represented by other family members. On the fifteenth, Cecil Beaton drove to Coppins to photograph the proud parents and their baby son, while two days earlier Queen Mary had spent the afternoon with George and Marina. The visit had clearly given her very great pleasure: 'The baby is sweet,' she noted in her diary later that day, 'Had luncheon & tea ... Walked in the garden – Georgie showed me some of his interesting things ... he looked so happy with his lovely wife & the dear baby.'

Not quite two weeks later, George, his private secretary Lieutenant John Lowther, his equerry Pilot Officer the Hon. Michael Strutt and his valet Leading Aircraftman John Hales prepared themselves for a visit to the RAF bases in Iceland. During the late afternoon of 24 August the duke said his farewells to Marina before driving himself up to London, where he boarded the overnight train for Inverness. It was the start of something that had its genesis in George's desire to play a more definite and necessary part in the war effort. His friendship with the Roosevelts and with the American-born Nancy, Viscountess Astor, the first woman to sit as a member of the British Parliament, and who had, indeed, introduced him to a number of senior US officers, helped to further his ambition of working as a liaison officer between the American and British air forces. Decisively, his actor friend Douglas Fairbanks Junior, then serving in the US Navy, arranged a meeting between George and General Carl 'Tooey' Spaatz, the first Chief of Staff of the United States Air Force. It was Spaatz who in May 1942 became commander of the Eighth Air Force who came up with the suggestion that George should fly to Iceland and once there find himself invited to a nearby US base. Spaatz would then officially request George's services as a liaison officer between the British and American bases.

As he stepped off the train at Inverness the following morning, 25 August, George was met by Group Captain Geoffrey Francis, Commanding Officer No. 4 (Coastal) Operational Training Unit at Invergordon, which would be the duke's point of departure. When he arrived at the base, George was introduced to the carefully selected team responsible for flying him to 'the frozen north', as he referred to his destination.

Leading the immensely experienced crew was Flight Lieutenant 42057 Frank McKenzie Goyen of Royal Air Force 228 Squadron. A 26-year-old Australian who had already flown Sir Stafford Cripps, Britain's ambassador to the Soviet Union, to Moscow, he had over 1,000 flying hours on ocean patrols to his credit. As captain, Goyen would fly the lumbering Sunderland flying boat W4026 DQ-M, which had been flown from Oban the previous weekend and was now moored on the Cromarty Firth, the surface of which looked as smooth as grey slate, as one observer described it that day. Sitting next to Frank Goyen on the flight and acting as first pilot would be Wing Commander Thomas L. Moseley, Commanding Officer of 228 Squadron, who was attached temporarily to the Sunderland's crew as a courtesy to the aircraft's royal passenger. Completing the flight personnel, all of whom had been personally selected by Moseley, were Pilot Officer Sidney Wood Smith, second pilot; Pilot Officer George Saunders, acting as Navigator; Flight Sergeants Charles Lewis, William Jones and

Ernest Hewerdine, and Sergeants Edward Blacklock, Arthur Catt and Leonard Sweett. Flight Sergeant Andrew Jack was to act as rear gunner.

On 25 August, while the crew was being briefed, the Duke of Kent and his party took lunch with Group Captain Francis. At about 12.30pm they were ferried out to the aircraft by marine tender. Once aboard, they spent the next half hour or so making the routine pre-flight checks of instruments, and generally warming the flying boat up ready for take-off. At about one o'clock the duke was welcomed on board, and it is thought most likely that he and his staff would have gone straight to the wardroom in the belly of the craft. Minutes later the Sunderland began to move across the waters of the Cromarty Firth, which were so calm that the flying-boat needed an unusually long run before finding a wave to help it lift off. Low cloud along the south coast of Caithness that day meant that flying conditions would be poor for the first part of the flight, but the general forecast was favourable with clearer weather expected to the north and out over the Atlantic.

At 1.10pm the Sunderland was airborne and, flying between the two precipitous headlands at the mouth of the Cromarty Firth known as the Sutors, turned north-east to follow the coastline. Inland from the east coast village of Berriedale, no more than thirty minutes later, David Morrison and his son Hugh were rounding up their flock of sheep when they heard the aircraft approach from the sea; though because of the dense mist – known in Scotland as 'haar' – neither father nor son were able to see it. Then followed the sound of an almighty explosion as the Sunderland crashed on a hillside and two and a half thousand gallons of aviation fuel blew up, sending a wall of flame skyward. Of the fifteen men on board, all but one was killed. The single, badly-burnt survivor was Andrew Jack, whose rear gun turret – ironically considered the most dangerous place to be – had broken off, hurling him to the ground.

In the past several writers have been under the common misapprehension that the Sunderland collided with Eagle's Rock, an 800-foot promontory on the Duke of Portland's Langwell estate. Others have claimed that it cleared the summit of the rock but ploughed into rising ground beyond. Research indicates that neither assumption is correct. For the aircraft to have encountered Eagle's Rock at all, it would have had to approach the hill from a different direction altogether, probably consistent with flying towards, not away from, Invergordon. What the Sunderland had in fact cleared, or had perhaps flown round, was the 2,000-foot summit of Meall Dhonuill, or Donald's Mount, situated at the eastern end of Scaraben, a ridge running east to west and lying south of Eagle's Rock itself. Having cleared Donald's Mount, however and, for some inexplicable reason in thick mist and hazardous terrain, the plane descended to an altitude of only 700 feet and thundered straight into the gently sloping hill which, at its western extreme, rises to Eagle's Rock.

At the sound of the explosion, Hugh Morrison sprinted downhill to the track where he had left his motorcycle and sped to the little community of Braemore to raise the alarm. He then rode on the coastal village of Dunbeath to alert the local physician, Doctor Kennedy, and the police. Immediately the first search party set out from Braemore, north-east of the site of the crash, while crofters and ghillies, who had also heard the news, set out from Berriedale. Later that afternoon the search parties discovered the wreckage and the bodies. From his house in Dunbeath, the elderly Doctor Kennedy and two special constables, one of whom was William Bethune, hastened to the scene. Both Kennedy and Bethune identified the Duke of Kent's body, still clad in his flying suit. Despite a severe gash to the head, his features were clearly discernible, though the inscription on his identity bracelet left nobody in any doubt. It read, 'His Royal Highness The Duke of Kent, "The Coppins", Iver, Buckinghamshire'.

At Coppins that evening, when the telephone rang, Marina had not long gone to her bedroom, intending to have an early night. Kate Fox, who had nursed the duchess as a baby thirty-six years earlier, and who had come out of retirement to help with the seven-week-old Prince Michael, took the call. Numb with shock, and no doubt wondering just how best to break the news, she slowly climbed the stairs. Hearing her old nurse's reluctant tread, it is said that Marina immediately sensed disaster, and the moment Foxy opened the door, cried out, 'It's George, isn't it?'

At Balmoral where members of the royal family were on holiday, the king and queen were having dinner with Harry and Alice, Duke and Duchess of Gloucester, when the steward entered the dining room and whispered to the king that Sir Archibald Sinclair, Secretary of State for

Air, was on the telephone and needed to speak to him urgently. When he rejoined his family, George VI was grim-faced and silent. The news, he later confided to his diary, 'came as a great shock to me, & I had to break it to Elizabeth, & Harry & Alice who were staying with us ... We left Balmoral in the evening for London.'

When the king was called from the table, the Duchess of Gloucester's first thoughts were of Queen Mary – that something had happened to her. In fact, the 75-year-old queen dowager, who spent the war years with her niece Mary, the Duchess of Beaufort and her husband at Badminton House in Gloucestershire, had spent the day in active high spirits. During the morning she had driven over to Lord Methuen's country house, Corsham Court, once owned by two of Henry VIII's wives, Catherine of Aragon and Katherine Parr, to attend a lecture and visit a picture gallery. She had then spent the rest of that wet afternoon at Badminton, putting photographs into her huge scarlet folio albums; and after tea had sat at her needlework, while Lady Cynthia Colville, one of her ladies-in-waiting, read to her. News of Georgie's death was received shortly after dinner. 'I felt so stunned by the shock,' Queen Mary wrote in her diary. 'I could not believe it.' Because of the close relationship she had always shared with her fourth son, the king's immediate thoughts were of his mother. On her part, Queen Mary's first thoughts were of her daughter-in-law. 'I must go to Marina tomorrow', she said and the following morning she climbed into her famous old Daimler and drove to Coppins. When she arrived, she found Marina in a pitifully desolate state; one moment sobbing uncontrollably, the next staring blankly into space, utterly motionless.

As the disaster made headline news around the world, tributes to Prince George flooded in. From Australia, where parliament was adjourned as a mark of respect, Premier John Curtin said that Australians 'had always highly regarded the duke, whose designation for the governor-generalship had evoked real pleasure'. In Victoria, the Greek community prepared a message of condolence for the duchess, in which they expressed their appreciation of the fact that Prince George had been a 'staunch supporter of our beloved and suffering country'. From Canada, Prime Minister Mackenzie King said of the duke, 'I greatly admired him for his public service and his attractive personality.' Further tributes were received from the presidents, governors-general and prime ministers of New Zealand, South Africa, Portugal, Argentina and China, while in the United States Senator Tom Connolly, Chairman of the Senate Foreign Relations Committee said, 'The Duke of Kent's brave conduct will serve as an inspiration to his gallant comrades in the armies and navies of the United Nations.'

More private messages were sent to the royal family by those who had ties of personal friendship. In a telegram to the widowed duchess President Roosevelt said, 'I am shocked beyond measure at hearing of the tragic accident and I want you to know that I feel the loss very deeply and personally. He has given his life for his Nation and in a great cause. I am thinking much of you and the babies.'

In response, Marina wired, 'Am deeply touched by your kind and understanding sympathy and your appreciation of my beloved husband. Am heartbroken.'

To Queen Mary, Roosevelt cabled, 'May I tell you of my great sorrow in hearing of the tragic accident to your gallant boy'; while to the king, his message read, 'I feel that I have lost an old and true friend and I want you to know how heartsick I am at this tragic accident. My wife and I are thinking much of all of you.'

Other friends were no less stunned. Noël Coward, who had many reasons for remembering Prince George with particular affection, wrote in his diary on 26 August, 'A dreadful morning. Headlines in the papers saying that the Duke of Kent was killed yesterday afternoon in an air crash. I can hardly believe it, but of course that is nonsense because I believe it only too well. It is never difficult to believe that someone young and charming and kind is dead. They are always dying .... Well, there goes a friendship of nineteen years. I shall miss him most horribly. He may have had his faults, but he was kind always and I feel absolutely miserable.... I am taking this resentfully and personally. I am so deeply sorry for the poor Duchess. I wrote to her this morning, of course, a rather inarticulate letter.... In memoriam I say, 'Thank you for your friendship for me over all these years and I shall never forget you.'

In Scotland on 27 August the body of the thirty-nine-year-old duke, contained in an oak coffin draped with the blue flag of the RAF, was taken from Dunrobin Castle, seat of the Duke of Sutherland, where aircraft-men had mounted an all-night vigil, to the local railway station. There the London-bound train made an extra stop and, as the guard-of-hon-our presented arms, and a crowd of local people wept openly, the coffin was borne to a special carriage and placed next to those of some of the Sunderland's other victims. Later that day, conveyed in a canvas-topped military ambulance, the duke's remains were taken by road from Euston Station to Windsor Castle, where they were placed in the ornate, marble-walled, Albert Memorial Chapel, near the tombs of two more princes who had died far too young, Queen Mary's first fiancé, Eddy, Prince Albert Victor, Duke of Clarence and Avondale, and Queen Victoria's eighth child and youngest son Prince Leopold, Duke of Albany.

When Marina arrived at the chapel shortly afterwards, clutching a small bunch of red and white roses which she had cut from bushes grown by Prince George in the garden at Coppins, she asked to be left entirely alone. Outside in the Galilee Porch, a stone passage that sepa-rates the Albert Memorial Chapel from St George's Chapel, the duchess's lady-in-waiting, Lady Herbert, waited for her together with officers of the Grenadier Guards. Next day she returned, a solitary black-veiled figure in the midst of a mass of colour – the chapel floor paved with veined marbles of various hue, the walls covered with panels of coloured marble designed by Baron Henri de Triqueti, depicting scenes from the Old Testament, and the vaulted roof gilded and set with Venetian glass mosaic; all an out-ward expression of an earlier inconsolable grief, that of Queen Victoria for her 42-year-old husband, Prince Albert.

The funeral of Prince George, Duke of Kent, took place in the cathedral-like St George's Chapel, dedicated to the Blessed Virgin Mary, St George and St Edward the Confessor, on the morning of Saturday 29 August. Supported by the queen and Queen Mary, Marina was escorted to her place opposite the purple catafalque near the high altar. Having come from the Albert Memorial Chapel, the cortège entered St George's to the hymn *Abide with Me*. Now draped with the duke's personal standard, on which was placed his Air Commodore's cap, together with Princess Marina's wreath of multi-coloured garden flowers arranged on a base of George's favourite clove carnations, the coffin was borne on the shoulders of four vice-marshals and two air marshals. Preceded by the Dean of Windsor, Dr Baillie, and by his equerries, Lieutenant-Colonel Humphrey Butler and Captain Lord Herbert – who carried the duke's insignia on crimson velvet cushions – the procession made its way along the nave and passing through the fan-vaulted organ screen into the Quire. As it approached, Marina's gaze never left her husband's gold-braided cap until the coffin was set down on the catafalque. She then knelt in prayer, and but for the moment when the duke's titles were proclaimed by Garter King of Arms, she remained kneeling throughout the service. At the end, the queen held her arm as she paused to look down into the open space into which her husband's coffin had descended into the royal vault. Then, as the organ played Chopin's *Funeral March*, followed by Christian Sinding's *Intermezzo No. 1*, a favourite piece of the duke's, Marina was led from St George's.

'I have attended very many family funerals in the Chapel,' King George VI wrote, 'but none ... have moved me in the same way.'

For Noël Coward, 'The service was impressive and supremely dignified. I tried hard not to cry, but it was useless. When the Duchess came in ... I broke a bit, and when the coffin passed with flowers from the garden at Coppins and Prince George's cap on it I was finished...

'After it was all over and the King had sprinkled the earth and the Royalties had gone away, we all went up one by one to the vault [shaft] and bowed and secretly said goodbye to him. Then we went out into the very strong sunlight. Margot Oxford [Countess of Oxford and Asquith] came up to me and said, 'Very well done, wasn't it?' as though she had been at a successful first night. I thought this offensive and unforgivable.'

By the time Queen Mary left Windsor to drive back to Badminton that afternoon, 'a fearful thunderstorm' had broken. Yet for that grand old dowager, the journey was not without diversion and, for a moment, her private sorrow was interrupted when she gave a lift – as she frequently did – to 'a charming young American parachutist', who was 'most friendly', and to 'a nice Sergeant Observer' from the Royal Air Force. Within a few days, Queen Mary had resumed what she called her 'wooding' activities, which meant sawing up logs and even trees in the grounds surrounding Badminton House. 'I am so glad I can take up my occupations again,' she wrote, 'Georgie wld have wished me to do so.'

On 14 September, three weeks after the crash, George VI drove from Balmoral to Berriedale to visit the site of his brother's death. By the time of his arrival most of the wreckage had already been removed. But only time and nature could erase every sign of the aircraft's devastating path; '... the ground for 200 yds long & 100yds wide had been scored and scorched by its trail & by flame. It hit one side of the slope, turned over in the air & slid down the other side on its back. The impact must have been terrific as the aircraft as an aircraft was unrecognisable when found.'

What exactly happened on the afternoon of Tuesday, 25 August 1942, some thirty minutes after take-off, remains one of the great mysteries in aviation history. Despite the fact that Prince George was one of the most important public figures to die in a wartime crash, a full explanation of the tragedy has never emerged and the same baffling question inevitably confronts those who probe the disaster. How could such an experienced crew at their most alert have made such a fatal error as to descend into low cloud when the established procedure under such conditions was to gain altitude?

Among those who made an in-depth study of the crash and its possible causes was the writer and broadcaster Robin Macwhirter, who during investigations for his BBC Radio programme *The Crash of W4026*, transmitted in August 1985, interviewed a number of people who remembered the crash or were in some way connected with it. They included Hugh Morrison, William Bethune and Jean Auld, a sister of the sole survivor, Andrew Jack. He subsequently met Group Captain Francis, who had been commanding officer at Invergordon. As Robin Macwhirter and others were to discover when examining the disaster, all documents pertaining to the official Court of Inquiry have apparently and remarkably vanished into thin air. The National Archives (Public Record Office), the RAF Historical Branch, and the Royal Archives at Windsor Castle all deny having possession of the key records relating directly to the death not of some obscure, insignificant princeling, but of the Duke of Kent, a senior-ranking member of the royal family, brother of the king, and at that time fifth in line to the throne.

To compound the mystery still further, the discovery that the flight briefing had also disappeared, again apparently without trace, means the route Flight Lieutenant Goyen and Wing Commander Moseley were instructed to follow remains open to conjecture. In an article published in the quarterly review *After the Battle*, David J. Smith, like Ralph Barker, author of *Great Mysteries of the Air*, points to the Sunderland having been instructed to take what might seem to be the most obvious route; that is to say, to follow the coastline in a north-easterly direction for some eighty to eighty-five miles, keeping out over the North Sea and turning through the Pentland Firth, on course for Reykjavik, the Icelandic capital. This, however, is by no means the only route the fated Sunderland may have been told to take. RAF personnel have explained that it was far from unusual for aircraft to gain a safe altitude of 4,000 feet over the Moray Firth, then turn inland at Dunbeath to fly over the predominantly flat landscape of Caithness to the Pentland Firth. Having interviewed local people who remembered the accident, Robin Macwhirter suggested that the Duke of Kent's aircraft flew up the coast and crossed inland at a point known as The Needle, just south of the Berriedale Water, and then flew up the wide river valley. It then cleared Donald's Mount at the eastern end of Scaraben and was heading north for the Pentland Firth when disaster struck.

Over the years, there have been many theories about the cause of the crash itself and why the Sunderland should have been flying as low as 700 feet at the time of impact. These have ranged from the effects of down-draught on the aircraft or the influence of magnetic rocks on its compasses to plain sabotage. Some of the suggestions seemed plausible enough, while others were little more than pure fantasy.

In the late 1930s, before the outbreak of war, King George VI, like countless other men and women of every class who had lived through the Great War, enthusiastically supported Prime Minister Neville Chamberlain's policies of appeasement. To that end the king had 'recruited' the Duke of Kent with his intimate family links, especially in Germany, where several relations were Nazi sympathizers and indeed members of the Nazi Party, as the ideal emissary 'uniquely placed,' as one observer put it, 'to act as an intermediary between high ranking Nazis and the movers and shakers of British society for the betterment of Anglo-German relations'.

With that in mind, it is perhaps unsurprising that the lexicon of theories surrounding George of Kent's fatal flight three years into the war, includes the suggestion (and there are other similar scenarios) that, having picked him up on a remote Scottish loch, the duke and Hitler's deputy, Rudolf Hess, were *en route* to Sweden as part of a top secret mission to broker a negotiated peace.

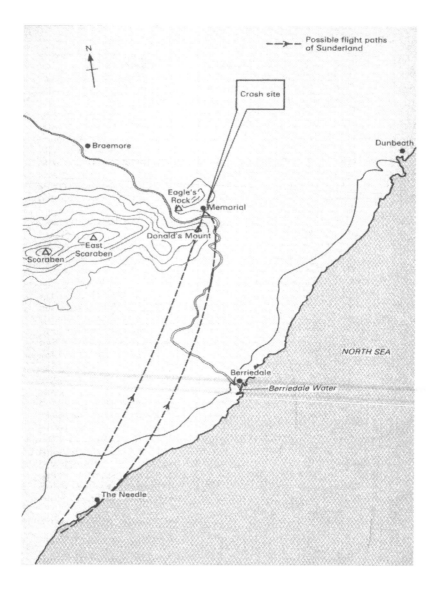

Theories aside, however, on 7 October 1942, Sir Archibald Sinclair, the Secretary of State for Air, reported the findings of the special Court of Inquiry to the House of Commons. According to the extract published in *Hansard*, 'The Court found: First, that the accident occurred because the aircraft was flown on a track other than that indicated in the flight plan given to the pilot, and at too low an altitude to clear the rising ground on the track; secondly, that the responsibility for this serious mistake in airmanship lies with the captain of the aircraft; thirdly, that the weather encountered should have presented no difficulties to an experienced pilot; fourthly, that the examination of the propellers showed that the engines were under power when the aircraft struck the ground, and fifthly ... that all the occupants of the aircraft were on duty at the time of the accident.'

In his article *The Tragedy at Eagle's Rock*, published in *The Scotsman* in August 1985 to complement transmission of his radio programme, Robin Macwhirter reacted to the claim that the accident was entirely the captain's fault by saying, 'If skipper Frank Goyen made such an elementary error as failing to seek altitude in bad visibility he wasn't alone in making that decision. Wing Commander T.L. Moseley, the CO of 228 Squadron, was seated beside him as first pilot for this special trip. Goyen also had a second pilot, a navigator and seven other men, engineers, radio operators, gunners watching what he was doing. All were men of experience, all men who valued their lives.'

CHAPTER FOURTEEN
MIN, EDDIE, PUDDING & MAOW

In its initial stages, the intensity of Marina's grief at Prince George's death was so acute that it caused much concern within the royal family. The king and queen did what they could, as did Queen Mary, even though it was she who lost no time in warning Marina not to surrender to self pity or to allow grief to overwhelm her. She had, said the queen dowager who knew all about putting duty first, a responsibility and a *duty* to every other war widow. Nobody but Queen Mary, who had of course lost a much loved son and was coping with her own grief, could have been as forthright and Marina understood what she had said. Nevertheless, in those first days and weeks, all attempts to reach the duchess in her misery were not helped by the palpable sense of distance that always existed between her and her husband's family – and for which Marina herself was entirely responsible. In the same way that Princess Nicholas was only too conscious of her heritage and position – and didn't let others forget it – so Marina was acutely aware of who she was, not just as Duchess of Kent, but more significantly, as a thoroughbred princess of both royal and *imperial* descent. As such, she exuded a distinct air of superiority. The result was that she was never properly absorbed into the British royal family, who, as Kenneth Rose the distinguished historian and Kent family friend put it, 'did not share her consciousness of royalty as a caste apart, or of a Europe composed more of dynasties than of nations.'

None of this is intended to imply that the duchess was not warmly regarded by members of the royal family. It was simply that through the divisive influences of background, intellect and cultivation, Marina never felt particularly close to her in-laws. Indeed, she resented the fact that both her sisters-in-law, Queen Elizabeth and Alice, Duchess of Gloucester, neither of whom were of royal birth - 'Och, those common little Scottish girls' she would say - held senior-ranking positions to her own. As time went by, it also became clear that there was no love lost between Marina and Queen Elizabeth. As Cecil Beaton would put it many years later, 'The Queen Mother adored Princess Marina the moment she died. When she was alive, she hated her!' Now, without George at her side, the divisions would become even more pronounced.

Impotent to penetrate the shadows surrounding the grieving duchess, George VI recognized that she needed to be comforted by a member of her own family. To that end he persuaded Churchill - despite anticipated opposition from within parliament and the press - to permit Princess Paul to come to England. Churchill gave his approval, the king sent a telegram to Kenya and on 10 September, accompanied by Madame Lilia Ralli, an old friend of Marina and herself, Princess Olga set out on a journey that took her through Uganda, the Cameroons, Nigeria and the West African coast to Portugal, from where she travelled to Ireland, thence across the Irish Sea to Poole Harbour in Dorset on England's south coast. Her circuitous route ended when she finally arrived at Coppins one week later. It was the first time that Olga and Marina had seen one another for more than two years and, given the extraordinary circumstances, it was an intensely emotional reunion.

It wasn't long, however, before the expected backlash to Princess Paul's presence began. Under protection of parliamentary privilege, Captain Alec Cunningham Reid, Tory MP for St Marylebone, stood up in the House of Commons and fired the first salvo in the slanderous campaign against the princess that would last for several weeks. Referring to Olga as a 'sinister woman', and strongly implying that she was a spy, Cunningham Reid finally demanded on 16 December, 'Has not this lady been allowed to be in a position whereby she will be able to convey information to her quisling husband which might be invaluable to the Axis?'

At that, the Foreign Secretary, Anthony Eden, leapt to his feet and sharply rounded on Captain Cunningham Reid. 'The circumstances are well known,' he countered. 'Princess Olga was the only sister of the

Duchess of Kent who could come to this country at all and she came here with the Government's authority and approval, and I have no apology to make in the matter.' When Eden had finished speaking, the entire House rang with cheers.

With her sister's support, Princess Marina's life began its slow return to some kind of recognizable form. Members of the royal family continued to drive over to Coppins, and old friends such as Chips Channon, Nancy Astor and 'Bobbety' Cranbourne, (later 5th Marquess of Salisbury) then Leader of the House of Lords, began paying afternoon visits. Lilia Ralli also proved diverting company, entertaining the royal sisters with amusing stories and shared reminiscences. By the end of September, Marina felt up to writing replies to some of the messages of sympathy she had received. On the twenty-ninth she picked up one of Cecil Beaton's photographs of George, Michael and herself, to send to President Roosevelt. In her distinguished, angular calligraphy, on black-edged writing paper embossed with her personal art-deco cipher, the duchess wrote, 'I want to send you this photograph of your God-son that was taken when he was six weeks old. It is the last one of my husband. I hope I will have the pleasure of introducing him to you in the not too distant future.'

Six weeks later, on 7 November, Queen Wilhelmina of the Netherlands sent Roosevelt her own impressions of Prince Michael. She wrote, 'I had to wait some time after the tragic death of Georgie Kent to go and see our godchild. Now I have just visited Marina and seen little Michael. He is such a darling, and he was in a very good temper, and has such a radiant laugh, and fine big blue eyes and much golden hair, that even stands up in a crest. I think he will later on much resemble his father.' In the event 'little Michael', like his sister Alexandra, grew to resemble Marina. Only Eddie, in almost every single respect, took after his father.

Within ten weeks of her husband's death Princess Marina put on her commandant's uniform to fulfil the first public engagement of her widowhood. On 4 November 1942, solemn but composed, she visited a Wren training centre in London. Writing to her mother-in-law Queen Elizabeth said, 'I have seen Marina ... several times ... [she] seems much better, and still very brave, & trying to take up the threads of her life again. Poor darling, one's heart aches for her in that little house, with such <u>very</u> lively children.' At the invitation of the king and queen, Birkhall, an 18th-century house on Royal Deeside (which is today home to the Prince of Wales and the Duchess of Cornwall) was put at Marina's disposal for summer holidays; a place where those 'lively' children could let off steam. Writing to Queen Mary from Balmoral in August 1944, the queen said, 'Marina seems very happy at Birkhall, & is out all day with the children. We have met for picnics, & she brought Eddy to lunch after church – he is a dear little boy, & much improved in manners. The children are well, and it is so nice to see very bright eyes and pink cheeks again.'

By the summer of 1944, Marina had become involved with some of the organizations with which Prince George had been actively associated. She had, for example, become patron of the Royal School for the Blind as well as the training ship *Arethusa,* a 4-mast naval frigate, moored at Upnor on the River Medway in Kent. Later still, in succession to the duke, she was appointed colonel-in-chief of the Royal West Kent Regiment (subsequently The Queen's Regiment), from which, on the day of Prince George's funeral, a battalion had been detailed to line the west aisle of St George's Chapel as part of the ceremonial guard-of-honour.

And it was to St George's Chapel, the magnificent church founded by Edward III five centuries earlier that the Duchess of Kent made a particularly poignant visit on 20 December 1942, the day that ought to have been her husband's fortieth birthday. Driving to Windsor, Marina climbed down the narrow winding staircase just beyond the tombs of Edward VII and Queen Alexandra to the royal vault, and there laid a wreath of clove carnations on her husband's coffin.

Eleven days later, on New Year's Eve, Princess Olga left England to return to Kenya, where Prince Paul now lay in a desperate state of ill health. Profoundly depressed by the fate of Yugoslavia, which Germany had ultimately invaded; the death of his brother-in-law and great friend Prince George, his wife's absence and Alec Cunningham-Reid's bitter invective of which he was well aware, the former Prince Regent took to his bed, rarely bothering to get up, refusing all offers of food, and drinking nothing more than a daily cup of hot chocolate. Hopes that Princess Olga's return might halt her husband's psychological decline were short-lived; so much so, that in February 1943 Prince Paul's doctors feared 'the development of insanity in the form of melancholia'. In London, Churchill continued to resist all petitions for the family to be allowed to move to South Africa, but in the end he was brought round. On 11 June (which was also Olga's fortieth birthday) Prince and Princess Paul with their sons Alexander and Nicholas and their daughter Elisabeth left Kenya for Johannesburg where, free from suspicion and no longer regarded as prisoners, Paul's health began to improve.'

For Marina, concern over her brother-in-law and the strain his condition imposed on her sister proved cathartic, helping to channel her thoughts in another direction. Work also continued to play a part in her recovery and, during 1943, the duchess made a full return to public life. In addition to the official duties which occupied her, Marina was to pay tribute to her late husband's pre-war work when she too became a factory inspector. Another tribute she paid to Prince George followed the royal tradition of leaving rooms and possessions undisturbed. In November 1942 the Channons spent a weekend at Coppins after which Chips noted, 'The Duchess has rearranged her sitting room, kept the Duke's just as it was, and has shut up the music room .... Went up to bed about midnight, and I was haunted by the spirit of the Duke. Every room and object is so inspired by him, the house, in fact, is him. I met him on the staircase, saw him sitting at the end of my bed, as he so often used to do, and was constantly aware of him. The house still vibrates with his vivacious personality.'

Coppins was now officially owned by Eddie. It had been left to him in trust until he came of age. Until he grew up and married, it of course remained very much Marina's home. Indeed, with the exception of a couple of rooms which her mother-in-law had put at her disposal at Marlborough House, Queen Mary's official London residence, Marina had no other.

When the Kents first moved to Iver, George – like Princess Victoria before him – had soon become a familiar figure in the village and, in time, Marina followed suit. Even today some of the local people remember how, when walking to St Peter's Church on a Sunday morning or pottering about the village, the duchess always 'had a smile and a "good morning" for everyone'. John Evans, who lived in Iver until 1956 and who, as a teenager, was the delivery boy for the local grocers, provided a brief glimpse into Marina's more domestic existence when he said 'I used to deliver groceries twice a week to the rear entrance of Coppins. I had an errand bike with a huge basket on the front. Prince Edward had a ride on it when he was quite young. The duchess, wearing an apron and a headscarf, was often in the kitchen, cooking. A few times on very hot days, she gave me a home-made ice-cream; a real treat for a wartime lad. She would always call me 'John' and ask about my family. I suppose even as a boy I was flattered ... but that's the kind of person she was. I believe the whole village loved and respected her. She was a grand lady.'

Home and family were always foremost features in Princess Marina's life. Her love for Eddie, Michael – or 'Maow', to rhyme with 'now' as he was known – and Alexandra, or 'Pudding' as the family called her during her adolescence, was total. Nevertheless as a parent, 'Min', the name by which Marina was known to her children and other members of the royal family, tempered indulgence with an insistence on strict discipline, good behaviour and impeccable manners. Even as adults, Eddie, Pudding and Maow ran the risk of incurring their mother's extreme displeasure by the slightest breach of this rigid code of conduct.

Another lesson the Duchess of Kent instilled in her children was the value of money. Nothing, she warned, would ever be theirs just for the asking. One example of this was provided by Clifford Wade who was for many years the local chemist in Iver. Eddie and Alexandra were regular visitors to his shop, and he recalled an occasion when they came in together to spend the first pocket money they had ever received. Between them they had exactly sixpence (otherwise half a shilling; 2½ pence today) and it was clear that neither really knew how wisely to spend it or on what. After some while, Clifford Wade heard a great deal of whispering and, looking up, saw the young duke and his sister arguing over a bar of highly perfumed soap. Eddie was heard to say they would never be able to use any soap other than that already in their bathroom; while Alexandra insisted they could easily smuggle it into the house without anyone finding out. She suggested that she could use it first and then surreptitiously pass it to Eddie when it was his bath time. Whether the ruse worked only they could say, but at all events, in what bordered on triumph, the children handed over their pocket money and gleefully marched out of the shop.

To Chips Channon, Princess Alexandra, gauche, gangly and full of energy, was 'a whirlwind of a girl.' Eddie was more diffident, hypersensitive and, on occasion, possessed of much the same bad temper as his father. Michael, on the other hand, while sharing his sister's more even temperament, was as reticent as his brother, perhaps even more so. Even as an adult in his early twenties living at Kensington Palace in London, he might ask one of his mother's footmen to accompany him to nearby St Mary Abbott's Church, just in case somebody should recognize him and stop to pass the time of day.

Towards the end of the war, one of Princess Marina's first considerations was fulfilling plans for her children's education. In 1943 Eddie had been sent to Ludgrove, a preparatory school near Wokingham in Berkshire. Five years later, as planned at the time of his birth, he went on to Eton, but by 1951 he had been removed from England's foremost public school, apparently for health reasons, and completed his education at Le Rosey, an internationally renowned boarding school on the shores of Lake Geneva in Rolle, Switzerland. Later on, he entered the Royal Military Academy at Sandhurst and was subsequently commissioned into the Royal Scots Dragoon Guards (Carabiniers and Greys).

Like Eddie, Prince Michael went first to a preparatory school, this time at Sunningdale, followed by Eton and then Sandhurst. After training with the Royal Armoured Corps at Bovington Camp in Dorset, 'Maow' was commissioned into the 11th Hussars, afterwards The Royal Hussars (Prince of Wales's Own).

Academic life for Alexandra was less rigorous. At the age of eleven she became the first British princess to attend boarding school. That chosen by her mother was Heathfield in North Ascot, run by Miss Kathleen Dodds, a young and progressive head teacher, who tended to concentrate on the overall development of her students as individuals rather than count the number of potential candidates for university. After Heathfield, the princess went to Paris where, during the winter of 1953-54, she stayed with the Comte de Paris and his family, before going on to finishing school. When she returned to London, Alexandra took a short nursing course at the Great Ormond Street Hospital for Sick Children.

However and wherever the children were educated, the Duchess of Kent had to meet the cost herself, and financially the ten years from 1943 to 1953 were difficult for her. During her brief married life neither she nor Prince George had any financial worries at all. Indeed, with a considerable private fortune of his own (he had, for example, inherited three quarters of a million pounds from his father) as well as a £25,000 annuity from the Civil List, with anticipated increases in the years ahead, life couldn't have looked rosier. In fact, in 1940 Prince George had even discussed selling Coppins and buying a much larger property in the Home Counties. When drawing up his will as a young man in his thirties, with a not unnatural expectation of a full life before him, therefore, the Duke of Kent left his personal wealth in trust for his children. When he died, however, his Civil List income died with him which meant that while she was scarcely destitute, the duchess had not been provided for. Contrary to George's belief, the Civil List at that time did not make provision for royal widows.

The result was that, no matter how 'humiliating', as she put it, Marina's only recourse was to sell off some of George's possessions in order to boost her capital and maintain a standard of living which, if not the equal of what she had become used to over the last eight years, would still be recognizable. The first sale, in November 1943, consisted of furniture left to Prince George by his great-aunt Princess Louise, Duchess of Argyll (Queen Victoria's fourth daughter), which, because he didn't want it, George had already decided to sell. At auction it realized almost £20,000. Four years later, in March 1947, a further £92,341 was raised when the duchess sent silver, furniture, pictures and porcelain to be auctioned at Christie's. Among the pictures she sold at this time were the celebrated Altieri Claudes, which sold for £5,300 and were bought by the American-born Huttleston Broughton, 1st Baron Fairhaven, to grace the walls of his country house Anglesey Abbey, near Cambridge.

To help out, both George VI and Queen Mary also provided the duchess with private – undisclosed – allowances. Later, following the sudden death of the king in February 1952 and the accession to the throne of his elder daughter as Queen Elizabeth II, the Civil List came under parliamentary review and was increased by £25,000. From that additional sum, although it did not amount to the full annuity Marina had been hoping to receive as a working member of the royal family, the new Queen officially allocated her aunt an allowance estimated at £5,000 a year. (In 2013 that sum equated to somewhere in the region of £400,000; and in the early 1950s, according to property advertisements of the time, £5,000 was still enough to buy a fine country house with considerable acreage).

It is undeniably true that, as a widow, Marina, Duchess of Kent – who left a relatively modest £54,121 net when she died – was never as excessively wealthy as many of her Windsor in-laws. But persistent claims that this princess, who knew all about thrift from her days as a Parisian exile, was 'hard up' or 'poverty-stricken' were very wide of the mark, especially when seen in relation to most people's lives. Not for them a four-storey, Wren-built, grace and favour house of upwards of twenty rooms at Apartment 1 Kensington Palace, or the services of a private secretary, ladies-in-waiting and office staff, to say nothing of a domestic household of a dozen paid servants, butler, under-butler, housekeeper, three footmen, two housemaids, a chef, a switchboard operator manning six lines and thirty extensions, and two chauffeurs to drive the duchess's dark blue 1951 Phantom IV Rolls-Royce (later exchanged for a larger, more modern model).

As an employer, Marina was very well regarded by her staff, even though she could seem rather imperious. As one footman recalled, she 'would never look directly at you when she spoke to you and she would never repeat an instruction'. But life below stairs at Number 1 Kensington Palace was not without amusement, as happened on one occasion when a newly-employed under butler was learning the ropes. As he was helping to prepare the breakfast things, the butler came into the kitchen announcing, 'Marina wants bacon' and on opening the fridge door added, 'and we haven't got any'. It was apparently not something she often asked for. Turning to the new under-butler, he said, 'Pop next door and see if they've got any.' In doing so, he saw an elderly woman at a downstairs window putting flowers in a vase. 'Marina wants bacon for breakfast and we haven't got any' he told her, 'have you?'

'I think we may have' she said, 'I'll have a look'. Minutes later she returned with a few rashers and the royal breakfast was duly served. Soon afterwards, when Marina was entertaining a few friends to tea, the very same under-butler found himself opening the front door to the very same elderly woman who had helped him out with the bacon. His look of astonishment greatly amused Princess Alice, Countess of Athlone who, putting her finger to her lips, whispered 'Ssshh, it'll be our little secret'.

It might also be borne in mind that throughout the twenty-six years of her widowhood whether in the salons at Kensington Palace or Coppins, Princess Marina continued to entertain in a way Prince George would have recognized. She made frequent trips abroad to family and friends and enjoyed regular skiing holidays; and where her wardrobe was concerned, though thorough in her costings which were always made in advance of any firm orders, she was never short of couture day and evening wear by designers such as John Cavanagh, Norman Hartnell and Victor Stiebel. At her death Marina bequeathed a magnificent collection of jewellery, diamonds, sapphires and pearls in the form of tiaras, necklaces, earrings, brooches, clips and bracelets to her daughter and daughter-in-law, with an additional provision for the future wife of Prince Michael.

Throughout the Second World War the Duchess of Kent's first cousin, Prince Philip of Greece and Denmark, the only son of her father's brother, Prince Andrew, served in the British Royal Navy. When not at sea the tall, blond, Nordic-looking prince was frequently to be found at Coppins. And when Philip was there, the King's elder daughter, Lilibet, as Princess Elizabeth was known within the family, was rarely very far away. Marina, who in 1944 had done much to further the romance between another of her cousins, Alexandra of Greece (posthumous daughter of King Alexander and Aspasia Manos) and King Peter II of Yugoslavia, for whom her brother-in-law Prince Paul had acted as regent, derived much pleasure at watching another and yet more significant courtship develop under her own roof.

For some considerable time Philip and Lilibet had waited for George VI to give his consent to their engagement, and in July 1947 he finally did. At their wedding in Westminster Abbey four months later, on 20 November, the eleven-year-old Princess Alexandra was one of her cousin's eight bridesmaids, while five-year-old Prince Michael and six-year-old

Prince William of Gloucester (who at thirty would also lose his life in an air crash) were Princess Elizabeth's page-boys or trainbearers. At the wedding rehearsal in the abbey, as Sir Michael Duff related to Cecil Beaton afterwards, 'Michael of Kent punched cousin William of Gloucester in the kisser ... which alarmed our Duchess [Marina] considerably, and he received a good talking to from Granny [Queen Mary], who with parasol in hand, was prepared for action should it occur on THE DAY.'

On THE DAY, the bride's bouquet went missing and the band of her diamond fringe tiara snapped, causing panic at the palace; but at Westminster Abbey the two young princes in their kilts and sporrans, patent buckled shoes and lace frilled silk shirts behaved themselves impeccably. At this – the last truly *royal* wedding Britain is ever likely to see, in that the bride and bridegroom were both royal highnesses by birth – a highly-excitable, eleven-year-old Alexandra, in her Hartnell-designed, star-spangled ivory tulle dress, also passed the ordeal with flying colours. A day or two later when she was back at school, however, she begged not to have to join a party of Heathfield girls on an outing to the cinema to watch a film of the royal wedding. With no wish to see herself on screen, she remonstrated that if made to go, she would die of embarrassment.

For the Duchess of Kent, the 1940s came to an end on a much happier note than they had begun. The war was over; she had accepted the loss of her husband; her home life, in spite of its inevitable changes, followed a comfortable pattern; her mother and sisters were again free, and as always, she was surrounded by friends who adored her. In 1948 Marina, who even during the war had featured regularly in newspapers and magazines though they were drastically reduced in size and content, was as newsworthy as ever, appearing at a variety of daytime events, gala functions, dinner parties and soirées in a way that was reminiscent of the days when she and Prince George as high society's most golden couple, dazzled London and with the Prince of Wales dominated the 1930s social scene. At the start of the year, the diary pages noted that the duchess had attended a service at St Mark's Church, North Audley Street in Mayfair, in remembrance of Mrs Laura Corrigan, American-born multi-millionairess, society hostess and one-time telephonist from Cleveland, Ohio. For the late Mrs Corrigan, rival of such famous hostesses as Lady (Emerald)

Cunard, a fellow American, and the Hon. Mrs Ronnie Greville who liked to boast of the number of red carpets she got through annually receiving royalty at Polesden Lacey, it was exactly the kind of tribute she would have revelled in; especially since the Duchess of Kent had never before attended a non-royal memorial service.

A little later, on 17 February, at a party given by Mrs Sacheverell Sitwell for the legendary Mae West, who was then appearing in *Diamond Lil* at the Prince of Wales Theatre, Marina not only met the star herself but also the comedian and movie actor Danny Kaye. On 1 March their paths crossed again. That evening Chips Channon, inveterate collector of crowned heads, princes and celebrities, gave an 'immense supper party' at his house in Belgrave Square, in honour of the 'mesmeric' Mr Kaye who was currently starring in his own show at the London Palladium. For the duchess and the celebrated entertainer, it was the start of a long and close friendship. Indeed, whenever he was in England, Kaye would invariably stay with Marina at Kensington Palace or Coppins.

Chapter Fifteen
A ROYAL PROPOSAL

Within the Duchess of Kent's circle, Lady Zia Wernher; Lilia Ralli, nick-named 'Figgi', because of her constant use of the expression *figure-toi*, ('just imagine'); Turia Campbell (born a Princess Galitzine); and Zoia Poklewska-Koziell and her mother, the biographer Baroness Agnes de Stoeckl, wife of a former diplomat and chamberlain at the Russian imperial court, were among her closest women friends. The baroness and her daughter even lived at Coppins Cottage on the duchess's estate. Though not all of them were able to claim imperial descent they nevertheless formed a kind of bridge that linked the nostalgic past with the sometimes more prosaic present.

Often they would gather informally round Marina's dining table, chat-tering, joking and exchanging the latest news of friends and relations scat-tered around the world. Cecil Beaton recalled that while Marina's parties 'lacked grandeur', they 'possessed a delightful atmosphere of the impromptu', usually accompanied by much hilarity. The duchess, said Beaton, 'loved to give herself up to uncontrollable laughter', adding that her amusement was sometimes 'caused by jokes of a quite basic nature.' Although the duchess herself abhorred and would never listen to gossip, particularly of a mali-cious or unkind nature, she not surprisingly regarded all conversations among trusted friends as strictly private. Indeed, the very moment the but-ler or a footman entered the room, Marina would stop speaking in English and without pause or hesitation switch to one of several languages common to her circle. Even between Marina and her sisters there was a language – hybrid Russian and Greek, perhaps – few admitted to having understood.

Through their professions other, predominantly male, friends – such as Noël Coward, Danny Kaye, Malcolm Sargent, Douglas Fairbanks Junior and Cecil Beaton – transported the arts-loving duchess to the world of entertainment. After the war Noël Coward became a regular escort, though theirs was not a friendship Queen Mary ever viewed favourably. More than once she wrote to her son's widow, indicating that she should end her relationship with a man who, in the dowager's opinion, was not quite the ticket. Marina's response was a resolute silence.

As with the diaries Coward kept during the 1930s and '40s, so his journals for the '50s and '60s were peppered with regular references to Princess Marina. On 25 June 1951, for instance, he noted, 'Went with the Duchess of Kent to Covent Garden to hear *Bohème* – Victoria de los Angeles sang well but looked like a musical bun ... Took the Duchess to dine at the Ivy, and then on to the Palladium for the Sid Field Benefit .... Highest spot – Judy Garland.' As the years passed there were many such references, some more fleeting than others, but always noted just the same: 'Lunched with the Duchess and Princess Alexandra', 'had tea with Princess Marina', and so on. Despite Queen Mary's disapproval Coward was a genuine friend who adored being with the duchess, whether entertaining her in lavish style or merely dropping in for a quiet chat over a drink or two.

Beyond Marina's personal friendships and the company she enjoyed in her private life, lay the inevitable responsibilities of her public role as one of the most popular members of the royal family. Of her official appointments referred to in an earlier chapter, one that always gave great pleasure was her presidency of the All England Lawn Tennis Club. Indeed, for many years, the princess's name was immediately synonymous with the world-famous tennis championships at Wimbledon which she attended every year and at the end of each tournament presented trophies to winners and losers on Centre Court.

Another organization to which she was dedicated was Alexandra Rose Day which, as noted earlier, had been established by her great-aunt Queen Alexandra. As president, Marina toured rose fairs and depots in London every year and on one occasion an incident occurred that continued to amuse long afterwards. Lady Constance Milnes-Gaskell who had been a Woman of the Bedchamber to Queen Mary for sixteen years, joined Lady Herbert and Lady Rachel Davidson (later Pepys) as a lady-in-waiting to

Princess Marina after the queen dowager died in March 1953. Whenever she went out with the queen, Lady Constance had always been used to walking round the back of the car to get in by the off-side door. It was evidently never done to climb across her Majesty. On the occasion in question, Princess Marina had taken leave of her hosts at a rose fair held at the Park Lane Hotel in Piccadilly and had settled herself in the back of her Rolls-Royce. As the car moved off, the princess leaned forward and asked Albert 'Bert' Jones, her chauffeur, 'Are we not taking Lady Constance with us on the rest of the tour?' Glancing in the rear-view mirror he was horrified to see the bewildered lady-in-waiting standing forlornly in the middle of the road. Not without some embarrassment, he slowly reversed the Rolls and picked her up. Amused though she was, Marina reproached Lady Constance, who was then in her late sixties and used to a very different protocol, 'You're not with Queen Mary now. You know, you really must remember to get in the same side as I do.'

Since the early days of her marriage the Duchess of Kent had maintained a full and comprehensive diary of official engagements in her own right. But with the start of the new reign in 1952, particularly at a time when there were far fewer members of the royal family than there are today, and no more than a handful of 'working' age, she was also asked to act as the Queen's representative abroad. The very first tour the duchess undertook was to Singapore, Malaya, Sarawak, North Borneo and Hong Kong. The idea for this particular five-week tour came when the duchess received an invitation on behalf of the Singapore Anti-Tuberculosis Association to open their new clinic. As president of the National Association for the Prevention of Tuberculosis in England, Marina had no hesitation in accepting. It was then that it was suggested that while in Singapore she might visit the Women's Royal Naval Service of which she was, of course, Commandant, and then as Colonel-in-Chief, fly to Kuala Lumpur in Malaya, to inspect the 1st Battalion, The Queen's Own Royal West Kent Regiment at Kuala Kubu Bahru.

Once the basic framework of the visit had been worked out, a further sixty-five official engagements were added to the duchess's schedule. Within three months her every move had been timed to the minute and on Saturday 27 September 1952, accompanied by Eddie, Marina left

London aboard the BOAC Argonaut aircraft *Atalanta* that had flown the then Princess Elizabeth to Kenya immediately prior to her unexpected accession to the throne eight months earlier.

With the duchess and the sixteen-year-old Duke of Kent travelled Lady Rachel Davidson and 'Johnnie' Althorp, otherwise Viscount Althorp, later 8th Earl Spencer, father of Diana, Princess of Wales, at that time an equerry to Elizabeth II, who had been seconded to the duchess's party. Another member of Marina's entourage was the swarthy Harrow and Cambridge educated Philip Hay who, at thirty-four, had been her private secretary since 1948, the year in which he married Lady Margaret Seymour, who had recently become a lady-in-waiting to Princess Elizabeth. Though he was described as handsome, civilized and cultured, Philip Hay was also abrasive. When receiving visitors who, in one way or another, had business with the Duchess of Kent, Sir Philip as he became would all too frequently follow a formal welcome with a terse 'I suppose you know why you are here?' There were, in fact, occasions when the visitor, having turned up only because he or she had been summoned, actually did not have a clue. But such was the brusque exterior of the man who was to serve Princess Marina for twenty years and whose relationship with her ultimately transcended the boundaries separating professional obligation and physical intimacy.

Hay also came to represent an important father-figure in the lives of Marina's children, especially to Prince Michael, whose interests he continued to manage long after his mother died. Later, Hay also became comptroller of the Duchess of Kent's household and as such was responsible for the sometimes difficult dealings with the Treasury and Inland Revenue over the duchess's income and expenditure and with the Foreign Office, Commonwealth Relations Office and what was then still known as the Colonial Office when it came to overseas tours, including that undertaken to the Far East by Princess Alexandra in 1961. With the itinerary carefully arranged, costed and agreed down to the last detail, Hay ruffled feathers when at the last minute the schedule was changed at enormous expense to the Colonial Office not only to enable the princess to stay with friends in Canada for three days on the way out, but also to visit ancient ruins in Aden on her way home.

In addition, a demand was made for a clothing allowance that would today be worth tens of thousands of pounds. A Treasury official noted, 'We are considerably perturbed at the way in which Sir Philip Hay has extended the itinerary originally agreed.... [He] said that the estimate for clothing was larger than anticipated because the princess would need two complete outfits – one for Far Eastern countries and another for the Canadian winter. It is difficult to see how the FO [Foreign Office] could be expected to bear the cost of a winter outfit for the princess to wear in Canada visiting private friends.' Hay himself evidently refused to provide itemized accounts, arguing instead that the British taxpayer was only 'making a contribution' to the royal expenditure. Small wonder, then, that Chips Channon was of the view that 'like all courtiers' Philip Hay was 'slowly becoming pompous'.

In September 1952, Hay was nevertheless at the Duchess of Kent's side when she and Eddie left Heathrow Airport at the start of their own tour of the Far East, flying south and then east to Rome, Cyprus and Bahrain (where they spent a few hours as the guests of Sheik Sulman bin Hamed al-Khalifah at his palace in Manama). They then flew on to Sri Lanka, then known as Ceylon, where the duchess and her son were welcomed by the Prime Minister, Dudley Senanayake, at the start of a twenty-four-hour visit to Colombo. The following day, as their aircraft approached Singapore, where the duchess received the freedom of the city, six Vampire jet fighters flew out to escort it to Kallang Airport. To the thud of a 21-gun salute, the *Atalanta* taxied to a halt in front of the guard-of-honour where, among the assorted dignitaries waiting to greet Marina and Eddie were John Fearns Nicoll, the governor of Singapore, and Malcolm MacDonald, commissioner-general for the United Kingdom in South-East Asia.

From the airport, the ducal cavalcade drove past thousands of flag-waving children towards Government House. Set in magnificent tropical gardens and resembling something that might have been erected in India during the days of the Raj, the mansion had been built in 1865 and had accommodated Queen Victoria's second son 'Affie', otherwise Prince Alfred, Duke of Edinburgh, during his empire tour four years later. From Government House the Duchess of Kent visited the Royal Naval base, the Admiralty Asian School, the University of Singapore, the 4th Independent

Company of the Women's Royal Army Corps and the British Military Hospital – and, she of course opened the anti-tuberculosis clinic that had first given rise to the idea of the tour.

On 5 October the royal visitors flew to Malaya, then still plagued by jungle warfare. On her way to the headquarters of the West Kent Regiment, in a tiny village forty miles from Kuala Lumpur, the duchess drove through terrain notorious for terrorist activity. In fact, on the day of the visit the Suffolk Regiment had shot and killed one terrorist, while troops and police had discovered slit trenches for fifty men overlooking the road, clearly indicating that the duchess's party was meant to have been ambushed. It was said that the would-be assassins had fled not more than three days earlier, after RAF strafing and regular army patrols.

By comparison, Princess Marina's visits to Sarawak and North Borneo were sedate affairs, though she did receive a deputation of Malay, Dyak, Melanaus, Kayan, Kenyah and Murut tribesmen, who had not long given up head-hunting in its most literal sense. As proof of his former occupation one Dyak headsman proudly showed the duchess a lock of hair he wore in his sword belt, telling her that it had come from the severed head of a Japanese officer unfortunate enough to have crossed the tribe's path. In North Borneo Marina's engagements included opening the recently completed barracks and police headquarters that were named in her honour, and the Duchess of Kent Hospital. Meanwhile, Eddie, who had celebrated his seventeenth birthday on 9 October, had been spending a couple of days up in the mountains with Bajau tribesmen hunting wild boar, though in the event, their only catch was a single civet cat. The tour continued with a visit to Brunei where the duchess and her son were greeted by the sultan, Omar Ali Saifuddin, and were carried to the sultan's palace in a state litter accompanied by an escort of staff carrying officials dressed in colourful silk outfits. At the oil town of Seria, the duchess was invited to christen the new oil well that had been named after her, which in traditional ship-launching style she did, carefully aiming a bottle of champagne at the narrow drilling bit. Brunei was followed by a five-day visit to Hong Kong and a schedule packed with inspections, openings, official receptions and formal dinners, before it was time to head back to England. Arriving at London Airport, Marina and Eddie, as was usual in those days, were met by a full reception committee; the Queen and the Duke of Edinburgh, the Queen Mother, Princess Margaret, the Duchess of Gloucester, Princess Alexandra and Prince Michael were all there to welcome them home. The duchess's tour had been a great success, not only from a personal point of view – the satisfaction of having accomplished her first overseas tour – but politically and diplomatically, too. Other official tours were to follow, among them Canada and the United States in 1954, when the duchess was accompanied by Alexandra, Latin America, again with her daughter who was proving herself every bit as popular with the public as her mother; Ghana at which Princess Marina represented the Queen at the country's independence celebrations, Australia, and Bechuanaland when it gained independence and became Botswana.

At the end of 1952, soon after she and Eddie returned from the Far East, the duchess and her children journeyed up to Norfolk to spend Christmas with other members of the royal family at Sandringham. That year, however, it was not without its sadder aspects. For Marina it would be the tenth Christmas to have passed without Prince George, but for her sister-in-law Elizabeth, the Queen Mother, it would be the first of fifty Christmases she would know without her husband 'Bertie', otherwise King George VI, who had died only ten months earlier in his ground-floor bedroom looking on to the pleached lime avenue and the North Garden that he had planted. Sometime later, Queen Elizabeth as she was still known within royal and court circles, commiserated with a recently widowed friend, 'I do hope Christmas time did not make you feel too sad. It is such a thing of memories I find, and one is thankful when it is over....'

By the time the royal family reassembled at Sandringham the following year, three more of its members would be absent. Marina's redoubtable mother-in-law Queen Mary had died at Marlborough House on 24 March 1953 at the age of eighty-five, and the new young Queen, whose coronation had taken place on 2 June, and her husband Philip, were away in New Zealand on the first phase of their epic six-month coronation tour of the Commonwealth.

By now Princess Marina was the only member of the small family into which she had been born still to be involved in royal duties. To all intents and purposes, the 71-year-old Princess Nicholas at home in her suburban villa in Athens, Olga and Paul now living in Paris, and 'Woolly' and Toto in their castle in Bavaria, were all private citizens. Long since freed of formal obligations, Olga and Paul were able to travel more or less whenever and wherever they chose. They would have liked to have settled permanently in Britain, but the war was still so recent and still so fresh in people's minds, that hostile public opinion meant it was not a serious option. The royal family, like Paul's other real friends, were never less than happy to see him. But the stigma of treason that he would nearly always wear when in England meant that he was regarded as an unwelcome visitor. As a visitor he came just the same, though in 1954 his presence was touched by tragedy. Five years earlier Paul and Olga's younger son Nicholas had followed in his father's footsteps to Christ Church, Oxford, and in 1952 had joined a city banking firm. On the night of 12 April (1954), the twenty-five-year-old prince, who had been to a party near Windsor, was heading back to London through nearby Datchet, when his sports car skidded, overturned, and threw Nicholas face down into a ditch. He drowned in a few inches of water. At Coppins, where the family was assembled - and where memories of Prince George's death must have returned to haunt her - Marina tried to comfort her sister and brother-in-law in their overwhelming grief. A few days later, Nicholas's funeral took place in the local church of St Peter in Iver. Throughout the night before Paul sat alone beside his son's coffin, while outside two policemen stood guard, a deterrent to reporters and any other unwanted visitors. Nicholas (who in October 2012 was finally re-interred along with his parents in the family mausoleum in Oplenac, in the small town of Topola in central Serbia), was first buried behind the church in the graveyard at St Peter's.

In the spring of 1954, the Duchess of Kent accepted the Queen's offer of a permanent London home, something that had become a consideration after Queen Mary died and Marlborough House, which had provided Marina with a base, was in the process of being dismantled as a royal residence. With Coppins a 40-mile (60 kilometre) round trip every time she attended a function in London, somewhere central became a necessity. As we saw earlier, what the duchess had been offered was an apartment at Kensington Palace. The term 'apartment', however, is misleading because it does not refer in any way to a 'flat', as is still frequently, but mistakenly assumed. At Kensington Palace, built by Sir Christopher Wren in the late 17th-century, the best description of a royal 'apartment' is a large (usually four-storey, basement to attic) red-brick terraced house in a quiet and highly exclusive compound. Indeed, the 'apartment' originally offered to Princess Marina occupied most of the south wing overlooking Kensington Gardens in one direction and the entire south-west corner, which was entered from a columned porte-cochère looking towards Kensington Palace Gardens, known today as 'Billionaires Row', across Palace Green, an expanse of lawn that at one time had been the parade ground. The last occupant of the property was Queen Victoria's fourth daughter Princess Louise and her husband, John Campbell, Marquess of Lorne, later the ninth Duke of Argyll. Princess Louise had use of the house, which encloses two sides of Clock Court – the largest of the three internal courtyards around which the palace was constructed – from the time of her marriage in 1871 until her death in 1939. Fifteen years later, the empty, dilapidated property was not only in need of renovation but in its entirety (there were more than forty rooms) proved much too big for the Duchess of Kent's requirements. The result was that the house was converted into two separate residences designated Apartment 1, which the duchess would occupy, and Apartment 1A. In 1962, again after greatly needed restoration, 1A became home to Princess Margaret and her then husband, the Earl of Snowdon. Today, it is occupied by the Duke and Duchess of Cambridge.

In 1954 the estimated cost for converting and renovating Apartment 1 was £80,000. In the event, the bill came to £127,000 and furious MPs demanded to know why, 'having regard to the urgent need for economy' the Government was prepared to foot the bill at a time when the country was still picking itself up after the war, and when fourteen years of food rationing (other restrictions had been gradually phased out) was only just coming to an end. Given that hard-pressed tax payers already contributed to the upkeep of the monarchy, it wasn't difficult to understand the strength of people's feelings on the matter. The Duchess of Kent, however, was deeply upset at the furore from both sides of the political divide, not least because if the fabric of an historically significant building was to be preserved and maintained as part of the national heritage, the work was a necessity not a luxury. In fact, there was much to be done at Kensington Palace as a whole. The north range of Clock Court and parts of the Queen's Apartments, as further examples, had been badly damaged by incendiary bombs in 1940, with the result that roofs and gaping window frames lay open to the elements and the inescapable effect of further decay and destruction. In the end, shortage of money and available materials meant that the long schedule of repairs to the palace would take over three decades to finally complete.

Despite the protests work on Apartment 1 went ahead and the duchess was finally able to move in on 21 October 1955; by which time the attention of both press and public was very firmly focused on the 'cliffhanger' outcome of Princess Margaret's romance with divorced war-time fighter pilot, Group Captain Peter Townsend and the question of whether they would or wouldn't marry.

During the eight years of the Kents' marriage, Marina as we know had always deferred to the personal taste, likes and dislikes of her husband. Since his death she had again become as assertive as she had once been. Now at Kensington Palace that assertiveness, which Prince George had at first put down as 'bossiness' was required to make the kinds of household decisions that had formerly been exclusively his.

In some respects, perhaps inevitably, the home Marina created at Apartment 1 reflected George's influence, though it essentially bore *her* stamp. From the main entrance, where the duchess always liked to keep fresh arrangements of yellow and white flowers, a long hallway (part of what had originally been the Stone Gallery, running the length of the south wing), led to a kind of inner hall where Marina hung a portrait of her mother by Philip de Laszlo, which had been given to Prince George and herself by Prince and Princess Christopher of Greece as a wedding present. Off to the right was a comfortable sitting room, from which French doors led down a flight of stone steps into a secluded walled garden. Beyond the staircase to the left of the inner hall was to be found the office Marina shared with Philip Hay, while next door was a large and splendid drawing room, with eighteenth-century furniture, fine pictures, country-house chintzes and a wealth of *objets d'art*, including pieces by Carl Fabergé, court jeweller to the Russian tsars Alexander III and Nicholas II. On the second floor were bedrooms and dressing rooms for Marina, Eddie (though as a serving officer he was away from home much of the time), Alexandra and Michael, together with guest rooms; while below in the basement were to be found the household offices.

Apartment 1 would be home to the Duchess of Kent for the next thirteen years. But had she ever considered re-marrying, she may not have stayed on at 'KP' as its residents refer to the palace, for very long at all. Indeed, had she accepted a proposal she received in the spring of 1957, she would have left England altogether for Oslo and a new life as queen of Norway. At that time, the fifty-four-year-old Crown Prince, who succeeded his father as King Olav V in September that year, had been a widower for three years; his wife Märtha, the daughter of Prince Carl of Sweden and Princess Ingeborg of Denmark, having died of cancer in April 1954. Since Crown Princess Märtha's death, Olav had been urged to marry again and the names of various suitable candidates had been suggested to him. Olav, however, was interested only in Marina of Kent.

By virtue of his birth line – his mother, Queen Maud, was the young-est of Edward VII and Queen Alexandra's three daughters; his father who became King Haakon VII of Norway, had been born Prince Carl of Denmark – Olav was extremely close to both the British and Danish royal families. It was therefore to his cousin Rico (who had by now succeeded to the Danish throne as King Frederick IX) that he turned in order to ask a special favour. Notwithstanding the delicate irony of the situation - it will be remembered that Rico had once been briefly engaged to Princess Marina's sister Olga – King Frederick agreed to act as Olav's go-between and in a manner that recalled the diplomatic preliminaries to arranged marriages in times past, flew to London. Over lunch he explained the nature of his visit to the Queen Mother who in turn was recruited to act as his special envoy. A few days later, 'the tea-cosy', as Marina and her family mischievously referred to Queen Elizabeth, invited her sister-in-law to lunch, during which of course the conversation gradually turned to Crown Prince Olav's proposal. Charmed though she was, the duchess nevertheless declined.

While stories that Marina and Olav were to marry had appeared in the press three years earlier, one of the most curious 'marriage' rumours of all first surfaced in October 1945, when the Belgian newspaper *Libre Belgique* claimed that the recently-widowed Duchess of Kent was to marry their very own regent, the forty-one-year-old Prince Charles. It was nothing more than empty speculation, but for some reason the Belgian press seemed anxious to marry their prince off to a member of the British royal family. After Marina, who was at least much the same age, the Belgians decided that Charles was about to become engaged to Princess Elizabeth, George VI's twenty-year-old daughter who, as it happened, was already deeply in love with Marina's cousin Philip of Greece.

Princess Marina's decision not to re-marry was in tribute both to Prince George and to their children. Yet even so, she neither disguised nor denied the need for a man in her life, though if for the most part their identities remain unknown it is for one very simple reason; that each of her relationships was conducted with the utmost discretion, one of the hallmarks of Marina's existence. That said it is an irrefutable fact that she and Sir Philip Hay, her private secretary, were lovers for many years. Another paramour was Sir Malcolm Sargent, the famous conductor and composer, who, according to his biographer Richard Aldous also had long-standing affairs with the Queen Mother's niece Diana Bowes Lyon and with Lord Mountbatten's wife, Edwina. It is believed (as his wife Angela publicly avowed), that Marina was also involved with the theatrical agent and serial philanderer, Robin Fox, father of the actors Edward and James, and grandfather of Emilia, Freddie and Laurence.

CHAPTER SIXTEEN
TOWARDS AN UNTROUBLED END

At the end of July 1955, Eddie, Marina's by now twenty-year-old elder son, graduated from the Royal Academy at Sandhurst as a Second Lieutenant in the Royal Scots Greys. It was the start of a military career that would span twenty-one years and would take him to Germany, Sierra Leone, Hong Kong and Cyprus where, in command of a squadron of his regiment he would serve as part of the United Nations force maintaining peace between the Turkish controlled area in the North of the island and the Greek controlled sector in the south. Over the years, Eddie would successfully climb the promotional ladder before finally retiring with the rank of Lieutenant-Colonel. He was subsequently elevated first to the rank of major-general and ultimately to field-marshal.

It was while stationed at Catterick garrison in North Yorkshire at the start of his career that Eddie first met his future wife. Almost three years his senior, Katharine Worsley was the only daughter of Sir William Worsley, Lord-Lieutenant of the North Riding, fourth baronet and squire of Hovingham Hall, an estate of over 4,000 acres, lying seventeen miles north of the city of York. The present hall, designed in the mid 18th-century by Thomas Worsley, George III's surveyor general, sits majestically on land the Worsley family has held since 1563. For the sports-minded, cricket matches have been held on the lawns at Hovingham since at least 1858 and it was Katharine's father who not only captained Yorkshire in the late 1920s, but was also president of the Yorkshire County Cricket Club for many years, playing host to such legendary players as Len Hutton, Freddie Truman and Geoff Boycott.

Descended from Sir Elias de Workesley, a Norman knight who accompanied Robert II of Normandy, the elder son of William the Conqueror, on the First Crusade, the family could also count Sir James Worsley, Keeper of the Wardrobe to Henry VIII, as well as that avowed anti-monarchist Oliver Cromwell, England's 1st Lord Protector, among their forebears.

Katharine's mother was Joyce Brunner, granddaughter of Sir John Brunner one of the two founding partners of the Cheshire-based chemical company Brunner Mond which, more than half a century later, became part of the global industrial combine ICI (Imperial Chemical Industries).

A pretty blonde in the mould of Grace Kelly, with a talent for playing the piano, organ and violin – in later life as 'Mrs Kent' she would become a music teacher at Wansbeck Primary, a state school for boys and girls in Kingston upon Hull, and would also establish the music charity *Future Talent* - Kate Worsley was working as a kindergarten teacher when she and Eddie's romance began. At around the same time, Eddie's sister Alexandra, whom it is said at one time hoped to marry the Irish peer Raymond O'Neill, stepson of James Bond creator Ian Fleming, had also met her future husband in the Honourable Angus Ogilvy, second son of the 12th Earl of Airlie (Lord Chamberlain to Queen Elizabeth the Queen Mother).

While her children were almost inevitably going to fly the nest at some stage, Marina, Duchess of Kent's attitude to that aspect of family life was ambivalent. For one thing, when Eddie married she would no longer be *the* Duchess of Kent, an idea that certainly did not please her; and though she took a fancy to one or two of Alexandra's boyfriends, personable young men from wealthy, aristocratic backgrounds, none in her eyes was right for her daughter. It was true, of course, that as a mother Marina wanted the very best for her children, but when it came to marriage the old business of 'caste' resurfaced and the 'very best', so far as the duchess was concerned, meant only one thing – *royal* marriages. For Eddie, Marina might have had in mind any one of several eligible princesses; Margrethe, elder daughter of Rico and Ingrid of Denmark, for instance, or her younger sister Benedikte. There was also Beatrix of the Netherlands, the eldest of her old friend Queen Juliana and Prince Bernhard's four daughters as well as her younger sister Irene.

For Alexandra, however, there was really only one decent catch: Harald of Norway. Oxford educated, he was the only son of Marina's one-time suitor King Olav, and it was well known in royal circles that the Duchess of Kent would like to have seen her daughter become crown princess – and eventually, like Prince George's aunt Maud many years before, queen – of Norway.

Dynastically, therefore, the marriages of her elder son and, when it came to it her daughter, too, were something of a disappointment. Yet, all the same they were going to happen, even if the duchess did wonder whether Kate Worsley was perhaps a little too old for Eddie or perhaps he was a little too young for marriage. Were they really right for one another? Such were the questions that occupied Marina's thoughts. After all, as Princess Alice, Countess of Athlone once put it – and she was to be proved right in several instances - only those who were *born* royal could really cope with what it meant to be part of the royal family and the responsibilities it entailed. Through uncertainty, therefore, Marina prevaricated, deliberately withholding consent to her son's marriage for almost three years. During that time, Eddie went away to Germany with his regiment and Katharine went to stay with her elder brother John and his wife Carolyn in Canada where, because of his business interests, they had set up home. When, after a year apart, Eddie and Kate both returned to England, their feelings for one another had withstood the test of enforced separation and Marina, who wistfully told a friend that 'it seems only the other day [Eddie] was a little boy,' finally gave them her blessing. On 8 March 1961, she formally announced Eddie and Kate's engagement in the usual way for these things via the Court Circular, which read: 'It is with the greatest pleasure that the Duchess of Kent announces the betrothal of her elder son, Prince Edward, Duke of Kent, to Katharine, only daughter of Sir William and Lady Worsley, to which union The Queen has gladly given her consent.'

When royal diaries were co-ordinated, Thursday, 8 June was chosen as the most convenient date for the wedding, which would take place not in London at Westminster Abbey as many had expected, but at York Minster. It would be the first royal wedding there since the Plantagenet king Edward III married Philippa of Hainault, daughter of William I, Count of Hainault, Holland and Zeeland, on 24 January 1328.

Another decision that had to be taken was who would be asked to design Katharine's wedding dress. Until now, Norman Hartnell, the doyen of royal couturiers, who had designed Princess Margaret's wedding dress only the previous year and who was the immediate choice when it came to grand royal occasions, usually received the royal summons.

On this occasion, however, the Duchess of Kent recommended John Cavanagh, the man who now made most of her outfits. He also designed for Princess Alexandra and in 1970, would provide many of the dresses Princess Anne took with her when she and Prince Charles accompanied the Queen and Prince Philip on an official tour of Australia and New Zealand. Reminiscing, Cavanagh recalled that Marina had told him that Katharine would like him to design her wedding dress and asked, 'Are you up to it?' By that she did not mean was he 'up to' designing the bridal gown, that was accepted without question, but more particularly did he feel able to cope with the inevitable and sometimes intrusive media interest, the pressure of a six-week time frame, for that is all there would be from commission to wedding day, and the additional requirement of designing and making the outfits both she and Princess Alexandra were to wear.

Unfazed, Cavanagh – who had begun his career, as he put it, 'picking up pins' for Edward Molyneux, the man who had designed Marina's wedding dress, and to whom he would become principal assistant – submitted five thumbnail sketch designs to the bride-to-be. At his salon in Curzon Street, Mayfair, he handpicked a small team of fitters and seamstresses and set aside a second-floor workroom in which, to discourage unwelcome attention, the windows were blacked out and the door, which he instructed was to be kept locked at all times, was reinforced with steel.

Once Katharine Worsley had chosen the design for her dress Cavanagh went in search of the right fabric. In France he found a shimmering white silk gauze woven with a pearlized motif. When it had been seen and approved by the bride, he placed an order for the 237 yards (just over 216 meters) that would make up the dress with its fitted bodice and stand-away collar, long sleeves, full skirt and 15-foot (4.57 meter) train. It was the train that initially caused Katharine and Marina some concern, for not only did the diaphanous skirt form its own train, but a second and still longer train fell from the waist. In terms of length and volume, it seemed to swamp the work room. Cavanagh calmed their anxieties by explaining that while it looked unmanageable in so limited a space its proportions would be reduced to the appropriate scale within the gothic immensity of York Minster.

With that out of the way, two further considerations needed to be dealt with. The first was how the fabric would behave during the ceremony when Katharine had to kneel and stand unaided. Producing a stack of telephone directories, John Cavanagh arranged them to the height of the prayer desk that she would use. Kneeling and standing, the silk gauze presented no problems. As she walked, however, it was discovered that the train pulled on the carpeted floor. At York Minster it would glide smoothly over the uncovered flagstoned nave, but would again drag on the carpets laid in the Sacrarium, and it was there that, at the end of the service, the new Duchess of Kent would have to curtsy to the Queen. As things stood the pull on the train meant she would not be able to do that as comfortably or gracefully as she would wish. Once again Cavanagh had the answer. As she approached Her Majesty, he said, Katharine should effect a half turn, step back into the folds of her gown, which would release the tension on the train and with head slightly bowed, perform her curtsy. There and then, Cavanagh offered Kate his arm, she curtsied and another problem had been resolved.

Three weeks before the wedding, the Duchess of Kent flew up to Scotland on an official engagement to inspect the Wrens at Lossiemouth on the Moray Firth. Forty miles away across the water, between the villages of Dunbeath and Berriedale, lay the site of the Sunderland flying boat disaster. On 16 May, Eddie and Alexandra joined their mother at the end of her visit to Lossiemouth, and together they made a private pilgrimage to the Celtic cross which serves as a memorial to Prince George, Frank Goyen, John Lowther, and the other men who died with them on that remote hillside on 25 August 1942. Marina had first visited the crash site in 1946 and had returned again on the tenth anniversary, in August 1952. This time, however, just ahead of such an important rite of passage in his eldest child's life, it was their way of paying tribute to Prince George, and their way of letting him know that at a time of family celebration he was never far from their thoughts.

On the day of the wedding itself, an almost typical June day of sunshine, rain and dark cloud, Marina - elegantly dressed by John Cavanagh in champagne silk organdie, and Alexandra in azalea pink – drove from Helmsley, some twenty-five miles from York, where they had been staying with friends, to the Cathedral Church of St Peter, as the Minster is properly known. Meanwhile, the Queen and Prince Philip together with the Prince of Wales, the Queen Mother, Princess Margaret, the Gloucesters with Prince William, Mary, Princess Royal, Princess Alice, Countess of Athlone, and a host of foreign royalties who had travelled up from London on the royal train, made their way to the Minster. It can have been the only time in its history that York Railway Station, its red-carpeted platform bordered on either side with banks of pink and blue hydrangeas, had welcomed so great a number of distinguished visitors on a single royal occasion.

A year before, in May 1960, when Princess Margaret had married fashion and society photographer Tony Armstrong-Jones, foreign royalty had been very conspicuous by their absence. Only Queen Ingrid of Denmark, Margaret's godmother had attended the Westminster Abbey wedding, along with a handful of minor German princes. The general feeling was that Princess Margaret had married beneath herself and Europe's ruling royal houses were all but unanimous in their reaction. Indeed, having lunched with the Duchess of Kent and Princess Alexandra, Noël Coward had noted in his diary, 'They are *not* pleased over Princess Margaret's engagement. There was a distinct *froideur* when I mentioned it.'

For Eddie's wedding, however, Europe's monarchies, past and present, would be well represented. Sitting with the British royal family were Marina's sister Olga ('Woolly' had died in 1955) and her husband Paul of Yugoslavia, and 'Cousin Ena', otherwise Queen Victoria Eugenia of Spain, behind whom sat her grandson Don Juan Carlos. A decade later, he would become Generalissimo Franco's nominated successor as Spanish head of state and upon his accession in 1975 to the restored Bourbon throne, the first reigning king since 1931. Sitting next to him that day in York Minster was Princess Sophia of Greece, the elder daughter of King Paul and Queen 'Freddie', whom he met for the very first time and would marry in Athens the following May, with Eddie's sister Alexandra among the bridesmaids. There too was Sophia's brother 'Tino', otherwise Crown Prince Constantine of the Hellenes, together with the heirs to the Danish and Norwegian thrones, Crown Princess Margrethe and Crown Prince Harald, Princess Irene of the Netherlands, Prince and Princess Frederick of Prussia, Prince Tomislav and Prince and Princess Alexander of Yugoslavia, and Prince Georg of Denmark and his wife Anne, a Bowes Lyon niece of the Queen Mother.

With Prince Michael beside him as best man, Eddie, Duke of Kent, wearing (by permission of the War Office) the famous scarlet, gold and navy ceremonial uniform of the Royal Scots Greys, with the star and rib-and of the GCVO (Knight Grand Cross of the Royal Victorian Order) across his tunic, awaited the arrival of his bride. To the sound of a trumpet fanfare Kate arrived a mere three minutes late and, as the choir sang Sir Hubert Parry's hymn *Laudate Dominum*, took her father's arm and walked slowly and with immense dignity along the nave towards the high altar, her face lightly veiled and a diamond bandeaux tiara, once owned by Queen Mary, catching the light of the television arc-lamps. Behind her walked her eleven attendants, three page boys in yellow silk jackets, white breeches and buckled patent shoes and eight bridesmaids, headed by Princess Anne, wearing rosebud trimmed 'Kate Greenaway' dresses of white silk with roses in their hair.

At precisely 2.50 that afternoon, Dr Michael Ramsay, Archbishop of York, soon to become archbishop of Canterbury, pronounced Edward and Katharine man and wife. At that moment, as they knelt in prayer, Marina ceased to be the Duchess of Kent. That distinction had now passed to her new daughter-in-law. With her son's marriage - and as the widow of a duke - Marina would in usual circumstances have become known as the Dowager Duchess of Kent. But 'dowager' was an ageing designation conjuring up images of white-haired old ladies in black satin and lace smelling of lavender. At not quite fifty-five, it was definitely not a title the stylish Marina intended to adopt. And, indeed, there was no necessity for her to do so. She had been born a princess with the rank of royal highness and that 'style' as it is known, was still hers by right. With the Queen's approval, therefore, she was now to be known officially as HRH Princess Marina, Duchess of Kent.

The loss of her position as duchess, however, brought with it a further painful deprivation in that Coppins would no longer be her country house. Eddie had inherited it from his father and it now became his and Katharine's married home. It meant that Kensington Palace would be Marina's only residence. Among those who knew her, some maintained that she felt bitter about the loss of her title and the house that she and Prince George had made their home a quarter of a century before. If that is true, then Marina bowed to the inevitable with grace and dignity.

Just over a year later, Eddie and Katharine became parents for the first time with the birth at Coppins on 26 June 1962, of a son who automatically assumed his father's subsidiary title, Earl of St Andrews. The arrival of her first grandchild was no less a significant milestone in Princess Marina's life, and on 14 September, she joined her family, together with Olga and Paul, the Worsleys, the Queen and Prince Philip and other members of the royal family in the Music Room at Buckingham Palace for the infant earl's christening. Dressed in the ivory satin and Honiton lace robe worn by all royal babies including his father and his aunt and uncle, since the days of Queen Victoria, George Philip Nicholas as he was named in honour of his grandfather, Prince George, his great-grandfather, Prince Nicholas of Greece, and his godfather, the Duke of Edinburgh, was christened by Dr Michael Ramsay, former Archbishop of York and now Archbishop of Canterbury, with water from the River Jordan, contained in the gold lily baptismal font that had been brought from Windsor for the occasion.

That November, Eddie was posted to Hong Kong with his regiment as second in command, and Kate and baby George joined him there. With them they took the family secret that would not be made public until 29 November - Marina's own twenty-eighth wedding anniversary – that Alexandra had become engaged to the Honourable Angus Ogilvy, an Eton and Oxford educated businessman, scion of the Airlie family and clan Ogilvy, and grandson of Queen Mary's old friend, Mabell, Countess of Airlie, in whom Prince George had long ago confided his desperate wish to leave the Royal Navy and join the civil service.

Like her parents, Princess Alexandra was married at Westminster Abbey and if anything there was even greater public enthusiasm for this wedding than there had been for her brother's two years earlier. The reason was that the good looking twenty-six-year-old princess, tall, elegant and very much her mother's daughter, was highly ranked on a very short list of most popular and approachable royal figures; bringing as she did a natural warmth and spontaneity to her official role.

As popular and well loved within the British royal family as with the general public at home as well as abroad, Alexandra was also highly regarded within the royal families of Europe and Scandinavia, to most of whom she was related. Indeed, if Eddie and Katharine's wedding had been well attended by foreign royal guests, the *Almanc de Gotha* would be even more in evidence at Alexandra's. Among those attending the celebrations were the bride's aunt and uncle, Olga and Paul of Yugoslavia, her cousin Countess Helen zu Toerring-Jettenbach (Woolly and Toto's daughter) and her husband Archduke Ferdinand of Austria; King Olav and Crown Prince Harald of Norway; Queen Ingrid of Denmark and her youngest daughter Anne-Marie, whom the following year would marry Constantine of the Hellenes, there with his mother Queen Frederica, his sisters Sophia and Irene, and Sophia's still relatively new husband, Juan Carlos of Spain; Queen Louise of Sweden with her step-granddaughters, the Princesses Margaretha and Desiree; the former queens Helen of Romania and Ena of Spain; Princess Irene of the Netherlands and her sister Margriet; the Duchess of Aosta; Prince and Princess Frederick Windisch-Graetz; Prince and Princess George of Hanover; and several princes and princesses of Hesse, Baden, and Hohenlohe-Langenburg.

At a floodlit Windsor Castle two days before the abbey wedding on Wednesday, 24 April 1963, royal guests, together with over a thousand others, attended a white tie and tiara ball which the Queen gave in honour of her cousin and which, in the Waterloo Chamber, turned into a ballroom for the night, Alexandra and Angus opened with a Strauss waltz. Five or six hours later, after more traditional dancing had given way to the rock 'n roll-inspired 'Twist', in which the Queen and Prince Philip also joined, the party began to break up, with Alexandra and Angus leaving the castle for the drive back to London not long before dawn.

Later the same day, while the princess and her fiancé gave a small reception at Kensington Palace for some of their overseas visitors, a final rehearsal for the bridesmaids and pages took place at Westminster Abbey, while the Queen, with King Olav sitting beside her and Prince Philip in the courier's seat, next to the driver, took the foreign royal wedding guests on a motor coach tour of Windsor Great Park and the surrounding Berkshire countryside, before ending up at the 15th-century Hind's Head in Bray for an up-market pub lunch.

That evening, while Angus Ogilvy hosted a dinner party for his family, Princess Alexandra stayed at home with her mother, sister-in-law and some close friends, enjoying a private 'hen night' celebration. Next morning, Alexandra was up early and although unable to eat any breakfast appeared to be the least nervous member of her family, telling them, 'Now let's keep calm and everything will be fine.' With the midday ceremony no more than a few hours away, one timely arrival at Kensington Palace was John Cavanagh, who was again responsible for designing the royal wedding dress. From the start Princess Alexandra knew exactly what she wanted; a classically simple lace dress with no bows, frills, flounces or unnecessary trimmings. To help him she entrusted Cavanagh with the lace veil that her second cousin, Lady Patricia Ramsay, the former Princess Patricia of Connaught, had worn at her own wedding at Westminster Abbey in 1919, and which she had given to Alexandra. Believed to have once been owned by Queen Charlotte, the old rectangular lace veil was much too old-fashioned to be worn by a modern royal bride, though because Alexandra liked its pattern of oak leaves and acorns, symbolic of strength and endurance (and in Greek mythology, very appropriately, the tree that is sacred to Zeus the king of the gods), she asked the designer if the motif could be replicated in the lace for her own gown. John Cavanagh entrusted the task to the same firm of French weavers that had made the silk gauze for the Duchess of Kent's wedding dress. He also came to an agreement with British Customs and Excise that when it arrived in England, the 80 yards of magnolia tinted lace would not have to be declared as such. To have done so would have been to tip off the press, some of whom had already attempted to bribe members of Cavanagh's staff for inside information.

In its simplicity, the wedding dress was everything Alexandra had hoped for, with a high round neck, wrist-length sleeves, fitted bodice and straight skirt forming a long train. The dress would be mounted on white tulle hand sewn with thousands of gold paillettes to add the slightest shimmer as she walked, while from her shoulders would fall a Court train, 21-feet (6.40 metres) in length, that would be edged with a border of antique Valenciennes lace that had belonged to Marina's mother, Princess Nicholas of Greece. During one of the final fittings, as Alexandra stood in front of a full-length mirror, John Cavanagh, who was standing behind her about to attach the Court train to her shoulders, suddenly had what he called 'a flash of inspiration' and suggested that the princess wear the train as her veil. It would, he said, be a first; never before had a royal bride worn a dress and veil of the same matching material. It was an idea that both Alexandra and her mother immediately liked with the result that earlier thoughts of a tulle veil were now forgotten.

By eleven o'clock on the morning of 24 April, as the bells of Westminster Abbey pealed out, most of the 2,000 guests had already arrived. Within another half hour the plethora of European royalty had taken their places and shortly afterwards the royal family and the Ogilvys had also been seated on opposite sides of the sacrarium. Nearby, Angus Ogilvy with his best man, fellow Scot and Second World War hero, the Hon. Peregrine Fairfax awaited Princess Alexandra's arrival. Also waiting for her at the West Door were her five bridesmaids in their Cavanagh-designed dresses of pale cream ziberline, who were again led by Princess Anne along with Ogilvy's niece Doune, and Helen and Ferdinand of Austria's effervescent six-year-old daughter, the blonde, blue-eyed Archduchess Elisabeth. With them were the two page boys and if the bridegroom himself had decided to wear morning dress (tail coat and striped trousers) instead of the kilt, his nephew, David, the Master of Ogilvy, and Simon Hay, son of Sir Philip, both wore the Ogilvy tartan.

Arriving at Westminster Abbey to a fanfare sounded by trumpeters of the Royal Military School of Music, Alexandra in her lace gown and wearing the diamond fringe tiara her mother had worn at her own wedding took Eddie's arm for the long and, because of the weight of her train, sedate walk along the blue-carpeted nave to the altar steps. For Princess Marina, wearing an elegantly exotic tunic dress of shimmering gold tissue embroidered with topaz and a cavalier-style hat covered with gold sequins, watching her only daughter become the Honourable Mrs Angus Ogilvy was a proud if deeply poignant moment. It was also one of overwhelming memories, for it was in that very same place that she and Prince George had knelt almost thirty years earlier and had been married according to the very same form of service that Alexandra and Angus now observed.

The royal wedding wasn't, of course, the only headlining event of 1963. It was also the year of the Great Train Robbery in Aylesbury, Buckinghamshire, of Martin Luther King's famous *I Have a Dream* speech on the steps of the Lincoln Memorial in Washington DC, of the election to the papal throne in Rome of Pope Paul VI, of John F. Kennedy's *Ich bin ein Berliner* speech in West Berlin, and the scandalous divorce proceedings of Ian Campbell, 11th Duke of Argyll and his duchess, one-time society beauty Margaret Wigham, whom Lord Wheatley, the presiding judge at Edinburgh's Court of Sessions, condemned as 'a completely promiscuous woman whose sexual appetite could only be satisfied with a number of men.'

Still more shocking and sensational than the Argyll's divorce, however, was the headline-hogging 'Profumo Affair' that was famously brought to trial at the Old Bailey. At the centre of the scandal were vicar's son Dr Stephen Ward, a well-known society osteopath; John Profumo, the Harrow and Oxford educated Minister of State for War and a Privy Councillor in the Conservative government of Harold Macmillan, and two Soho cabaret showgirls, Christine Keeler and Mandy Rice-Davies who were the chief witnesses for the prosecution. In their book *An Affair of State*, Philip Knightley and Caroline Kennedy reminded us that, 'Stephen Ward [whom Lord Denning at the time Master of the Rolls and the second most senior judge in England and Wales, described as the 'most evil man' he had ever met] was a central figure in the political scandal which shook Britain. It was in Ward's flat that John Profumo ... used to meet ... Christine Keeler. It was Ward who introduced Christine to the dashing Soviet diplomat, Yevgeny Ivanov. It was Ward who told MI5 about Profumo because he thought that their affair might pose a security risk. When Profumo lied to the House of Commons about his love life, and the resulting scandal threatened to bring down the Government, it was Ward who stood in the dock ... scapegoat for the establishment.'

As Ward was hung out to dry – and for weeks society talked of nothing else - so his friends, including the rich and famous through whose lives he breezed, abandoned him. As well as practising osteopathy, Ward had studied art on a part-time basis at the Slade School and it was as a portraitist that he undertook regular commissions for the *Illustrated London News*. Working in charcoal and pastel he provided the popular weekly news magazine with a number of drawings of members of the royal family. Like the Duke of Edinburgh, Princess Margaret, Eddie and Katharine, Mary, Princess Royal and the Gloucesters, Princess Marina was among his sitters. Hers, Ward said afterwards, was the most difficult likeness to capture because 'the mouth is ever so slightly askew, the sort of thing in a drawing that is extremely hard not to overdo. The result didn't please me and I don't think it pleased her.'

What pleased Marina even less was seeing her old friend John Profumo mired and humiliated by scandal, even if he had nobody but himself to blame for his downfall. In June he resigned both as Minister of War and as a Member of Parliament and though there were those who disowned him and his wife, the former film actress Valerie Hobson, Princess Marina was not of their number. All the same, there was one occasion during that summer of 1963 on which she cancelled an engagement with them. On 3 August, as the trial at the Old Bailey was about to be concluded and sentences passed, the Profumos were to have dined with Marina at Kensington Palace. But that day Stephen Ward, who had 'swallowed enough Nembutal tablets to kill a horse', died at St Stephen's Hospital in Fulham. As soon as she heard, the princess cancelled her dinner party and perhaps feeling the need to breathe fresher air left London for a few days in Scotland.

Come autumn, Marina had other more positive things to think about much closer to home. For by then it had been confirmed that Alexandra and Katharine were both pregnant with their first and second children respectively. To add to the celebratory mood, it had been announced that the Queen and Princess Margaret were also anticipating the proverbial patter of tiny feet, with the birth of each member of the royal quartet expected the following spring. Alexandra, who had fallen pregnant just weeks after she and Angus married, led the way when she gave birth to a son, James, on Leap Year's Day, 29 February 1964, followed by the Queen, whose fourth and youngest child, Edward, was born on 10 March. Katharine gave birth to a daughter whom she and Eddie named Helen on

28 April, and three days later, on 1 May, Princess Margaret was delivered of her second child, also a daughter, Sarah. While each of these events naturally gave rise to celebration – and for Marina there was the additional pleasure, even the novelty, of having become a grandmother for the second and third time in the space of only eight weeks – there were other occasions within her extended family to look forward to. In September 1964, for example, there was the wedding at the Metropolitan Cathedral in Athens of Tino of the Hellenes, who on the death of his father King Paul six months earlier had succeeded as King Constantine II, and the eighteen-year-old Princess Anne-Marie of Denmark, to whom he had become engaged two years earlier.

As events of this kind invariably did – and frequently still do - the wedding of King Constantine, who at the age of only twenty-four was Europe's youngest reigning monarch, brought together a host of royalty from around the world. With her cousin, Philip, Duke of Edinburgh, Prince Charles and Princess Anne (who was to be one of the bridesmaids), Marina flew out to Athens where she was joined by her sister Olga for the wedding festivities. Eighteen months later, Amsterdam was the setting of another royal wedding when, on 10 March 1966, Crown Princess Beatrix of the Netherlands, the eldest of Marina's old friend Queen Juliana's four daughters, married German-born diplomat, Claus von Amsberg. The wedding - which Princess Alexandra who was a witness at the couple's obligatory civil ceremony attended with Marina - was made the more newsworthy because of street protests and disturbances, including smoke bombs thrown at the bride's gilded coach, on the part of an organization known as 'Provo'. A short-lived 'counterculture movement', its members were vehemently opposed to Beatrix marrying a former Wermacht conscript, little more than twenty years after the country had been invaded and occupied by German troops for the duration of the Second World War.

At 'Trix' and Claus's wedding, Princess Alexandra was already five months' pregnant with her second child; and it was at Thatched House Lodge, the Georgian house in Richmond Park that Angus Ogilvy had leased from the Crown shortly before he and Alexandra were married, that a daughter was born on 31 July. At her christening at the Chapel

Royal, St James's Palace, a few weeks later, on 9 November, the baby was named Marina in honour of her grandmother.

If family had always played a vital part in Princess Marina's life, her official activities, her 'work', also provided an important focus. In September and October, not long before the christening of her second granddaughter, Princess Marina had again been asked to represent the Queen at celebrations marking the independence of countries that had formerly come under British rule. Flying out to South Africa, she was present at ceremonies marking the transformation of the former British Protectorate of Bechuanaland into the Republic of Botswana, and Basutoland into the kingdom of Lesotho. At home, she continued her support for each of the organizations with which she was connected, ranging from the newest - she had become the first Chancellor of the newly established University of Kent in 1966 - to the oldest, among which were the Royal National Lifeboat Institution, the WRNS, whose Golden Jubilee reunion she attended at the Royal Festival Hall in July 1967, and, of course, the Wimbledon tennis championships at which, shortly after her return from Copenhagen, where she had attended the wedding of Crown Princess Margrethe of Denmark to French diplomat Henri de Laborde de Monpezat, she presented the trophies on Centre Court to John Newcombe and Billie Jean King, that year's winners of the Men's and Women's Singles Finals respectively.

It was also during the summer of 1967 that Princess Marina joined other members of the royal family for what, although an official public engagement, was very much a family occasion - the unveiling by the Queen of a memorial plaque to Queen Mary on the garden wall of Marlborough House. Of grey slate it had been commissioned to commemorate the centenary of her birth. Incorporating a medallion profile portrait of Queen Mary in bas relief, the plaque was the work of Sir William Reid Dick, who had sculpted the full length statue of King George V that stands outside Westminster Abbey facing the Houses of Parliament.

Significantly, an invitation to attend the ceremony on 7 June, which was watched by crowds of onlookers, had also been extended by the Queen not only to her uncle the Duke of Windsor, as the elder of Queen Mary's two surviving sons, but also to his wife, Wallis. It was an historic moment, not least because the Duchess of Windsor, whom Queen Mary referred to at the time of the Abdication as an 'Adventuress', had never before been invited to a royal event, public or private, much less one in the presence of the Queen and, more especially, the Queen Mother, who was always regarded as Wallis's most bitter opponent.

From Claridge's, where they were staying, the Duke and Duchess of Windsor drove in one of the official claret and black Rolls-Royce limousines that had been sent from the Royal Mews, to the blue-carpeted dais on the corner of Marlborough Road and the Mall. As she took her place next to the duke, the stylish duchess in her slim-fitting navy blue coat and white mink scarf, a small navy straw pillbox hat perched on her immaculately coiffured hair, eclipsed every one of her royal in-laws, including the elegant Princess Marina herself.

After the ceremony, on what was Derby Day, a sacrosanct event in the royal racing calendar and one that was rarely if ever missed, the Queen with Prince Philip, the Queen Mother and the Duke and Duchess of Gloucester (the duke, otherwise Prince Henry, was the younger of Queen Mary's surviving sons), left immediately for Epsom. The Windsors did not go with them. Instead, 'David' and 'Wallis', who had celebrated their thirtieth wedding anniversary four days earlier, joined Marina, Eddie, Katharine and Michael for lunch at Kensington Palace. Whatever the rights and wrongs of the Abdication and the grievances some members of the royal family harboured in its aftermath, Princess Marina, who never forgot how close Prince George had been to his eldest brother, was determined that neither she nor her children should lose touch with the Windsors and they never did.

Fourteen months later, the duke would return to England for an occasion nobody could have anticipated. The year 1968 had started quietly enough with Marina and Michael eagerly looking forward to the private three-week safari they took together in Kenya, Uganda and Tanzania. Later, during the summer, Marina also planned to visit Olga and Paul at their villa near Florence, as she usually did. But then, on 19 July, for the first time in more than thirty years, the princess had to pull out of an official engagement. That afternoon, she had been due to visit the Frimley and Camberley Cadet Corps, but because of what was officially described as 'a slight knee injury', she had to ask Alexandra to go in her place. The truth was that for a while now Marina had been troubled by her left leg which would suddenly give way without warning causing her to stumble and fall. It wasn't long before the weakness also affected her left arm. Although she was only sixty-one, she made light of it, joking that it was all due to the advance of old age. 'We all grow old and we must face it,' she had said in a recent speech. 'For whatever our misfortunes have been, the disabilities and infirmities of old age are universal.' Universal or not, old age was not something Marina herself was looking forward to, though in the end it didn't matter.

At Kensington Palace on 18 July, the day before she was due to visit Camberley, Princess Marina fell badly and was admitted for tests to the National Hospital for Nervous Diseases. A day or two later, under firm instructions to rest, she returned home. What she would never know – and Eddie, Alexandra and Michael were to keep the agonizingly painful secret strictly between them – was that the tests had revealed an inoperable brain tumour. The prognosis was that at the very most the princess had no more than six or seven months to live.

On the day she returned from hospital Noël Coward visited her for tea. 'She was in bed and looked very papery,' he confided to his diary. 'I am worried about her. She was very cheerful, however, and we gossiped and giggled.' A few weeks later, on Friday, 23 August, Marina drove out to Richmond Park where she, Alexandra and the grandchildren spent two and a half hours sitting together in the garden at Thatched House Lodge. The following Sunday, which happened to be the twenty-sixth anniversary of Prince George's death, Alexandra and Angus joined Marina and her old friend Zoia Poklewska for an informal lunch at Kensington Palace. That evening, the princess suffered a black out. By nine o'clock the following morning she had drifted into an untroubled sleep. A little later, the Archbishop of Canterbury, Dr Ramsay, drove over from Lambeth Palace and spent a quarter of an hour praying with the princess's family in her bedroom. At 11.40am next day, Tuesday, 27 August, without having regained consciousness, Princess Marina, Duchess of Kent, died. Her sons and her daughter, as well as her son- and daughter-in-law were at her bedside, as was her sister Olga, who had arrived from Italy the day before, having received Alexandra's urgent telephone call.

Officially announced at 12.05pm, after the Queen who was on holiday at Balmoral, and the rest of the royal family, had been informed, news of Princess Marina's death was flashed around the world; television and radio programmes were interrupted, flags were lowered to half-mast, and the front pages of the evening papers, like those the following day, carried banner headlines. To her family who knew only too well that it would happen at some point during the next six months, but who could not have imagined it would be over in a mere five weeks, the sudden-ness of Marina's death came as a devastating shock. For them, the only consolation was that in other circumstances the princess had been spared a prolonged and debilitating illness. Indeed, in response to his message of sympathy, Princess Alexandra wrote to Cecil Beaton, 'Thank God my sweet Mama knew no pain or suffering. And now she is at peace.'

At Windsor Castle at about 6pm on 29 August, the same date on which his funeral had taken place in 1942, Prince George's coffin was brought up from the royal vault beneath the Albert Memorial Chapel (adjacent to St George's Chapel). Then, as residents drew their curtains, as they had previously been instructed to do, it was placed in a hearse and driven up through the castle's precincts and along the winding, tree-lined 'red brick road', as it is known, to Frogmore, the thirty-three acre estate acquired by George III that is part of the private Home Park. To the immediate north-west of the lake, behind the mausoleum which Queen Victoria had built for Prince Albert and where she too is interred, lies the Royal Burial Ground. Since it was consecrated in 1928, members of the royal family have been buried there in an immaculate garden setting; and it was there that two new graves had been dug side by side. Prince George's remains were lowered into one of them.

The following morning, 30 August, royal relations began arriving at Heathrow ahead of the funeral that afternoon. Among them were the Duke of Windsor, whom Eddie met on his arrival from Paris; Queen Juliana of the Netherlands; King Constantine and Queen Anne-Marie of the Hellenes, who now lived in Rome, whence they had fled in April

1967 after a group of right-wing army officers staged a coup d'etat; Tino's mother, the dowager Queen Frederika, Queen Helen of Romania, ex-king Umberto of Italy and the Duke of Edinburgh's sister, Princess Margarita of Hohenlohe-Langenburg.

At Windsor Castle meanwhile, non-commissioned officers of The Queen's Regiment, the Devonshire and Dorset Regiment, and the Corps of Royal Electrical and Mechanical Engineers who would act as pall-bearers for their royal colonel-in-chief, rehearsed carrying a dummy coffin up and down the triple flight of stone steps at the west door of St George's Chapel. Inside, beneath the magnificent fan vaulted roof, Princess Marina's oak coffin covered with a Royal Standard and the white and blue Greek flag, on which were placed wreaths of red, pink and yellow roses from the grown-up children she had known as 'Eddie', 'Pudding' and 'Maow', and of blue and white flowers from Olga and Paul, lay on a catafalque flanked by flickering candles.

A few hours later as the funeral began with the choristers singing the Sentences *I am the resurrection and the life*, the royal family walked behind the coffin into the Choir, aglow with heraldic devices and the colourful banners of the Knights of the Garter. During the service which was conducted by the Archbishop of Canterbury and the Dean of Windsor, the Rt Rev. Robin Woods, afterwards Bishop of Worcester, the impressive presence of the black-robed Archimandrite Gregory Theodorus, Chancellor of the Diocese of Thyateira, as well as the inclusion of the collect hymn of the Holy Orthodox Church, *Give Rest, O Christ to Thy Servant with Thy Saints*, was a reminder that while Princess Marina frequently worshipped at the Anglican parish church of St Mary Abbots near her home at Kensington Palace, she had always remained a member of the Greek Orthodox Church. Presently, as the service came to a close and the notes of Sir Henry Walford-Davies' anthem *God Be in my Head* faded away, the Duke of Kent, Princess Alexandra and Prince Michael held hands as they followed their mother's coffin towards the west door. Just before they stepped outside, however, they let go. It had been a private moment between grieving siblings, but it was also a reminder that royal figures do not betray private emotions in public.

As the family looked on the military pall-bearers successfully negotiated the west steps and with well-rehearsed precision placed the lead-lined coffin they had borne on their shoulders inside the waiting hearse. Minutes later, following the solitary route Prince George's remains had taken early the previous evening, the cortège left the chapel's Horseshoe Cloisters on its way to Frogmore, where Princess Marina was laid to rest next to her husband.

Like her marriage to Prince George – a fleeting 'once upon a time' moment in 20th-century British royal history – Princess Marina's life was to be a relatively short one. But as the then Dean of Westminster, Dr Eric Abbott, said in his address to a congregation of 2,000 at the princess's televised memorial service in Westminster Abbey on 25 October 1968, she had not only made England her home, but for over thirty years had given to it 'unswerving service'.

With her death, it is no exaggeration to say that the country Princess Marina had adopted as her own had lost one of its most highly respected public figures. Moreover, the nobility she brought to the royal family in terms of her royal and imperial heritage has never been and is unlikely ever to be equalled.

BIBLIOGRAPHY

Airlie, Mabell, Countess of, *Thatched with Gold*, Hutchinson, London, 1962

Aldous, Richard, *Tunes of Glory: The Life of Malcolm Sargent*, Hutchinson, London, 2001

Aronson, Theo, *Royal Family: Years of Transition*, John Murray, London, 1983

Balfour, Neil, and Mackay, Sally, *Paul of Yugoslavia*, Hamish Hamilton, London, 1980

Bloch, Michael, *The Duke of Windsor's War*, Weidenfeld & Nicolson, London, 1982

Bryan, J., and Murphy, Charles J.V., *The Windsor Story*, Granada, London, 1979

Buckle, Richard (ed), *Self-Portrait with Friends: The Selected Diaries of Cecil Beaton, 1926-74*, Weidenfeld & Nicolson, London, 1979

Christopher of Greece, Prince, *Memoirs*, Hurst & Blackett, London, 1938

Coward, Noël, *The Noël Coward Diaries*, Weidenfeld & Nicolson, London, 1979

Duff, David, *Hessian Tapestry*, Frederick Muller, London, 1967

Eade, Philip, *Young Prince Philip*, Harper Press, London, 2011

Ellis, Jennifer, *The Duchess of Kent*, Odham Press, London, 1952

Ellison, Grace, *The Life Story of Princess Marina*, Heinemann, London, 1934

Fox, James, *White Mischief*, Penguin, London, 1984

Gloucester, Princess Alice, Duchess of *Memories of Ninety Years*, Collins & Brown, London, 1991

Harewood, Lord, *The Tongs and the Bones*, Weidenfeld & Nicolson, London, 1981

Kennett, Audrey and Victor, *The Palaces of Leningrad,* Thames & Hudson, London, 1973

King, Stella, *Princess Marina: Her Life and Times,* Cassell, London, 1969

Knightley, Philip, and Kennedy, Caroline, *An Affair of State,* Jonathan Cape, London, 1987

Marlborough, Laura, Duchess of, *Laughter from a Cloud,* Weidenfeld & Nicolson, London, 1980

Massie, Robert K., *Nicholas and Alexandra,* Victor Gollancz, London, 1972

Morrah, Dermot, *Princess Elizabeth,* Odhams Press Ltd., London, 1947

Mortimer, Penelope, *Queen Elizabeth: A Life of the Queen Mother,* Penguin, London, 1987

Nicholas of Greece, Prince, *My Fifty Years,* Hutchinson, London, 1926

Ometev, Boris, and Stuart, John, *St Petersburg: Portrait of an Imperial City,* Cassell, London, 1990

Packard, Anne, *HRH The Duchess of Kent,* Pitkin, London, 1950

Petropoulos, Jonathan, *Royals and The Reich,* Oxford University Press, Oxford, 2006

Pope-Hennessey, James, *Queen Mary,* George Allen & Unwin, London, 1959

Rhodes James, Robert (ed), *Chips: The Diaries of Sir Henry Channon,* Weidenfeld & Nicolson, London, 1967

Rose, Kenneth, *King George V,* Weidenfeld & Nicolson, London, 1983

Rose, Kenneth, *Kings, Queens and Courtiers,* Weidenfeld & Nicolson, London, 1985

Shawcross, William (ed), *Counting One's Blessings, The Selected Letters of Queen Elizabeth The Queen Mother,* Macmillan, London, 2012

Strong, Roy, *The Royal Portraits,* Thames & Hudson, London, 1988

Thornton, Michael, *Royal Feud,* Pan, London, 1985

Vickers, Hugo, *Cecil Beaton,* Weidenfeld & Nicolson, London, 1985

Vickers, Hugo, *Elizabeth, The Queen Mother,* Hutchinson, London, 2005

Von der Hoven, Baroness Helena, *The Duchess of Kent,* Cassell, London, 1937

Vorres, Ian, *The Last Grand Duchess,* Hutchinson, London, 1964

Warwick, Christopher, *Two Centuries of Royal Weddings,* Arthur Barker, London, 1980

Warwick, Christopher, *Abdication*, Sidgwick & Jackson, London, 1986

Warwick, Christopher, *Ella, Princess Saint & Martyr*, John Wiley & Sons, Chichester, 2006

Watson, Sophia, *Marina: The Story of a Princess*, Weidenfeld & Nicolson, London, 1994

Wentworth-Day, James, *HRH Princess Marina, Duchess of Kent*, Robert Hale, London, 1962

Wheeler-Bennett, John W., *King George VI*, Macmillan, London, 1958

Whiting, Audrey, *The Kents*, Hutchinson, London, 1985

Williams, Susan, *The People's King*, Allen Lane, London, 2003

Wilson, Christopher, *Revealed: The Secret Illegitimate Brother of The Queen's Cousin*, Mail Online, 12 July 2013

Wilson, Christopher, *King George VII? Palace Plotters would have kept the Queen from the Throne*, Mail Online, 26 December 2008

Windsor, The Duchess of, *The Heart Has its Reasons*, Michael Joseph, London, 1956

Windsor, HRH The Duke of, *A King's Story*, Cassell, London, 1951

Young, Kenneth (ed), *The Diaries of Sir Robert Bruce-Lockhart 1915-1938*, Macmillan, London, 1973

Zeepvat, Charlotte, *From Cradle to Crown*, Sutton Publishing, Gloucestershire, 2006

Newspapers and magazines: *Daily Express, Daily Mail, Daily Telegraph, Evening News, Evening Standard, Illustrated London News, Manchester Guardian, Pitkin Pictorial Booklets, The Sphere, Sunday Dispatch, Sunday Express, The Sunday Times, The Times, Vogue.*

37093002R00105

Made in the USA
San Bernardino, CA
09 August 2016